# Social Movements

# Social Movements

*A Cognitive Approach*

Ron Eyerman and Andrew Jamison

The Pennsylvania State University Press
University Park, Pennsylvania

Copyright © 1991 by Ron Eyerman and Andrew Jamison

First published in the United States by the Pennsylvania State University Press, Suite C, 820 North University Drive, University Park, PA 16802

Second printing, 1996

ISBN 0–271–00752–4
ISBN 0–271–00756–7 (pbk)

*Library of Congress Cataloging-in-Publication Data*

Eyerman, Ron.
    Social movements : a cognitive approach / Ron Eyerman and Andrew Jamison.
        p.      cm.
    Includes bibliographical references and index.
    ISBN 0–271–00752–4 (alk. paper)
    ISBN 0–271–00756–7 (pbk. : alk. paper)
    1. Social movements.    2. Social movements—United States—Case studies.    I. Jamison, Andrew.    II. Title.
HN17.5.E99    1991
303.48′4—dc20

90–21197
CIP

Typeset in 10½/12 pt Times
by Graphicraft Typesetters Ltd., Hong Kong
Printed in Great Britain
by T.J. Press, Padstow, Cornwall

# Contents

*To B. R. with thanks*

# Introduction

In recent years, social movements have become a popular subject of sociological investigation. The civil rights movement of the 1950s and 1960s, the student movement of the 1960s and 1970s, and the various movements of the 1970s and 1980s have brought social movements into society to such an extent that sociologists can no longer avoid studying them. What earlier generations of sociologists analyzed as a special variety of "collective behavior" or as processes of social and political revolution has blossomed into an object of specialization on its own.

The ways in which social movements have come to be conceptualized, however, have made it difficult, if not impossible, to understand them. For like the understanding of most social phenomena, the understanding of social movements has come to be subjected to the whims of the academic marketplace. Sociology has provided a number of mutually irreconcilable modes of understanding social movements, what the philosophers call incommensurable explanations.

This response to social movements on the part of sociology follows a longstanding scientific tradition to divide and conquer, to break reality down into its component parts so as to be better able to control it. Science has largely become a process of reduction and objectification, and "truth" is seen as coming from distancing the subjective observer from the objects of investigation. In the social sciences, the pursuit of objectivity can be seen to have political, as well as intellectual, motivations. The rise of modernity and the differentiation of society lead to a form of social domination in which power has come to be based on the authority of scientific expertise. At the same time, the enlightenment ideal of science – to provide human beings with reliable knowledge as a means toward self-understanding – has been undermined. Science, as many contemporary observers have noted, has become an integral part of the exercise of political control (Aronowitz 1988).

The differentiation of society is reflected in sociology in the subdivision into academic specializations and the fragmentation of understanding that goes with it. The study of social movements is a particularly telling example of this process. From the original formulations in the 1930s and 1940s sociologists have conceptualized social movements either as isolated, particular social phenomena or as epiphenomenal expressions of deeper structural strain in the social "system", or – as a third "middle range" variant – institutionalized social actors mobilizing supporters for political purposes. Sociology has reinforced the divisions of modern society by imposing its own disciplinary division of labor onto social movements. Social movements are conceptualized as external objects to be understood in terms of pre-existing frameworks of interpretation. The sociology of social movements thus provides a kind of knowledge that can be useful for the preservation of the established political order rather than for its critical transformation. In the name of scientific progress, sociologists of social movements serve to tame social movements. By bringing them under academic control, however, they perhaps unwittingly serve to bring them under political control as well.

Our ambition is to go beyond the partial understandings provided by the sociology of social movements and provide an alternative reading. Our cognitive approach, as we will be presenting it in the course of this volume, offers a form of analysis that seeks to study social movements in their own terms. This does not mean that we take the actors' perspective, that we replace a naive objectivism with an equally misguided subjectivism. Rather, it means that we look at social movements through the complex lens of a social theory of knowledge that is both historically and politically informed. Although our perspective will unfold gradually, it can be helpful to provide the reader with some initial guidelines.

On the one hand, we view social movements as processes in formation. We study them as forms of activity by which individuals create new kinds of social identities. All social life can be seen as a combination of action and construction, forms of practical activity that are informed by some underlying project. Most often implicitly and even unconsciously, social action is conditioned by the actors' own "frames of reference" in constant interaction with the social environment or context. Action is neither predetermined nor completely self-willed; its meaning is derived from the context in which it is carried out and the understanding that actors bring to it and/or derive from it. By using the term cognitive praxis, we want to emphasize the creative role of consciousness and cognition in all human action, individual and collective.

The cognitive praxis that concerns us in this book is that which transforms groups of individuals into social movements, that which gives social movements their particular meaning or consciousness. What we call the dimensions of cognitive praxis are the relations to knowledge that characterize particular social movements, the concepts, ideas and intellectual activities that give them their cognitive identity. By knowledge, we mean both the worldview assumptions, the ideas about the world that are shared by participants in social movements, as well as the specific topics or issues that movements are created around. Movements are interested in knowledge in a variety of ways, which we identify as the different dimensions of their cognitive praxis. At the same time, movements are of interest for theorists of knowledge as providing the breeding ground for innovations in thought as well as in the social organization of thought. For us, social movements are bearers of new ideas, and have often been the sources of scientific theories and of whole scientific fields, as well as new political and social identities. By studying the processes by which these new ideas are formulated and then "taken over" by the surrounding society, we aim to make a contribution to the social understanding of knowledge production. By characterizing the ways in which individual "movement intellectuals" are formed and, in turn, re-form the cognitive identity of social movements, we also aim to contribute to the social theory of intellectuals.

Another characteristic of our approach is that it seeks to place social movements in political historical context. For one thing, we want to understand social movements in relation to their particular time and place, which means that we want to connect the study of social movements to a (contextual) theory of social change. Our approach is thus comparative, defining success or failure of social movements in comparative terms, both between historical periods and between political cultures. Social movements are, for us, transitory, historical phenomena, and their "success," as we will argue, is thus paradoxical. The more successful a social movement is in spreading its knowledge interests or diffusing its consciousness, the less successful it is likely to be as a permanent organization. Indeed, the longer a social movement continues to exist, as it were, "outside" of the established political culture, the less influence it is likely to have on the development of knowledge.

Social movements are thus best conceived of as temporary public spaces, as moments of collective creation that provide societies with ideas, identities, and even ideals. This is, of course, not to claim that all new ideas grow out of social movements or that all social movements are "progressive," but it is to give social movements a far different, and far more important significance than is usually the case.[1]

We conceive of social movements as forms of cognitive praxis which are shaped by both external and internal political processes. Social movements express shifts in the consciousness of actors as they are articulated in the interactions between activists and their opposition(s) in historically situated political and cultural contexts. The content of this consciousness, what we call the cognitive praxis of a movement, is thus socially conditioned: it depends upon the conceptualization of a problem which is bound by the concerns of historically situated actors and on the reactions of their opponents. In other words, social movements are the result of an interactional process which centers around the articulation of a collective identity and which occurs within the boundaries of a particular society. Our approach thus focuses upon the process of articulating a movement identity (cognitive praxis), on the actors taking part in this process (movement intellectuals), and on the contexts of articulation (political cultures and institutions).

The approach will be presented in the following manner. In the next chapter, we critically review the sociological study of social movements. Our ambition is to place the contemporary perspectives and approaches in context, and this in three main ways. First we want to indicate how the recent debates are derived from earlier traditions within the discipline, and beyond that from earlier approaches to social theorizing. Second, we want to show how the study of social movements is conditioned by the societal context, and especially by the role that social movements play in those contexts. Third, we want to explore the relation between the sociological study of social movements and the sociologist's conception of his/her own sociological role.

The chapter begins with a brief history of the main sociological points of departure, indicating how the initial concern with social movements among sociologists emerged from the experiences of the fascist and communist movements of the interwar years. The conceptualizations of the 1950s could, however, not respond satisfactorily to the student revolts of the 1960s; and we go on to portray the sociological study of social movements as an extended reaction to the coming of the "new social movements." At the end of the chapter, we will sketch out our own constructive alternative, which will be presented in more detail in the following chapters.

Chapter 2 develops the concept of cognitive praxis, placing it within the context of the sociology of knowledge and the history and philosophy of science. We want to show how an understanding of social movements as cognitive actors builds on perspectives emerging in the social study of science, in particular the focus on knowledge production as a form of social action. We also indicate the sources of our own contextual approach in the new social history of science, and beyond that, the sociological conceptions of knowledge that have developed since the nineteenth century.

The explicit attempts to create a sociology of knowledge and a critical theory of society in the 1920s and 1930s developed in relation to the then contemporary social movements of fascism and communism. The "escape from reason" so characteristic of interwar social movements led sociologists to formulate new ideas about the sociological conditioning of knowledge that were neglected after the Second World War. As with the study of social movements themselves, the movements of the 1960s "rediscovered" this sociologizing of knowledge. Our cognitive approach to social movements is thus an attempt to recombine the cognitive praxis of the 1960s student movement, which has been separated, over the past 20 years, into particular sociological specializations. We conclude chapter 2 on a methodological note.

Chapter 3 begins by discussing more explicitly how we have operationalized our concepts so that they can be used in actual sociological research. In what way can the sociologist uncover the cognitive praxis of a social movement? We attempt to answer that question by placing the concept of cognitive praxis in its own context. We briefly discuss the "epistemological" and historical significance of our concept. We show how the term builds on the earlier conceptualization of knowledge-constitutive interests (Habermas 1972) which Jürgen Habermas developed in his critique of positivism in the 1960s. In applying the term to social movements, however, we have made a contextual "translation" of Habermas's transcendental categories into levels or dimensions of historically contingent forms of praxis.

We then develop our central concepts through illustrative ex-emplification. In chapter 3, we disclose the dimensions of cognitive praxis in the environmental movement and then in the working-class movements of the nineteenth century. We indicate how our cognitive approach to social movements brings out a historical significance that previous accounts have not sufficiently empha-sized. In chapter 4, we elucidate the concept of movement intellec-tual, moving both phenomenologically and historically at one and the same time. The very idea of an intellectual, we contend, is the outcome of social movements, but we correct the static, even ahis-torical connotation that the idea has since taken on in sociology to make our own distinction between nineteenth-century *intellectuals in movements* and twentieth-century *movement intellectuals*. Our exploration of the various roles that intellectuals have played in historical and contemporary movements points again to the import-ance of context and of history in reading the underlying meaning of social movements.

In chapter 5, we present a cognitive reading, by means of these concepts, of the American civil rights movement. Here, we focus directly on the ways in which political culture and institutional traditions condition the development of social movements. The civil rights movement is, in many ways, a transition between the old social movements of the working class and the new social move-ments of postmodernism. It shared with the working-class move-ment a desire for inclusion into the modern industrial welfare state, but it also came to transcend that role by articulating new needs and desires which entered into a new wave of social movements in the 1960s and 1970s. Our analysis tries to show how the civil rights movement was formed by the historical and political context of Amercan society post-World War Two, a peculiar society in which the main divisions were not along class lines, as in Europe, but along ethnic and racial lines. As such, it was as a movement for racial equality that the universal challenge to the inequities of modern society took shape in the United States; and because that movement drew on cultural traditions and types of knowledge that were so central to the American national identity, the movement could lead to a fundamental questioning of the entire society. The national context thus provided the movement with its particular content – but also with its particular limitations.

We read the civil rights movement as shaped by context, but also as a reflection of a more general, even universal, feature of contemporary social movements. What began in the civil rights movement was namely the transcendence of "material" or industrial values by a new set of postmaterial values which constituted the cognitive identity of the student revolts of the late 1960s and came to be specified by the new social movements of the 1970s. These differences between modernist and postmodernist social movements are then explored more systematically in chapter 7.

It is important to state at the outset that our approach to social movements is selective. We have not attempted to explain all social movements or even to claim that our conceptualization is appropriate for all cases. We would make the much more modest claim that a cognitive approach can enrich understanding of social movements, and places at least some social movements in a very different historical and sociological light. It is of little importance to us whether all social movements can be said to have a cognitive praxis or whether all social movements are best approached cognitively. We do indicate that many significant social movements can be explored through our cognitive perspective, and we certainly contend that our approach could and should be applied to many other movements than we have been able to examine here. We have tried to be selective in an interesting way. The civil rights movement and the working-class movements of the nineteenth century are fundamentally different from the environmental movement which was the basis of our own empirical research. While not perhaps fulfilling the criteria for "ideal typical" status, these movements are nonetheless different enough to make generalization possible. At the very least our examples give ample basis for claiming that our terms, which emerged in our studies of the contemporary environmental movement (Jamison et al., 1990) can be applied to other social movements. We return to these questions in the final chapters where we also reflect on the future of social movements.

Since contextual conditioning plays such an important role in our approach, it might be useful to say something very briefly about the contexts that have served to shape this book. As we suggest in chapter 1, conceptualizations are conditioned by three kinds of contexts – intellectual, political cultural and personal. It is thus impendent on us to reflect on our own contextual frameworks in a more systematic and self-conscious manner before proceeding further. Intellectually, the book reflects and ambition to combine what are now separate discourses in the social sciences, namely critical Marxism and academic sociology. The ambition to read social movements cognitively is, more specifically, an attempt to link social theory with theory of science; we want to return to the original Enlightenment ideal of social science, to be found among other places in the writings of Marx and Weber, to think about society as the creative construction of human beings. We see that construction not as the work of elites, as Weber; rather, with Marx, we want to see it as the work of collectivities, of social movements.

Politically and culturally, our approach grows out of our status as émigré Americans in Europe. Conditioned by the American society of the 1950s and 1960s, we were both formed – at slightly different points in the social hierarchy – in the context of the civil rights movement and the war in Vietnam. Social movements, for us, are thus archetypically the emotional outbursts of our youth; and although the European varieties that we have studied in the years since we emigrated have been, in many ways, far different from the movements of the American 1960s, we have sought to read them – and interpret them – in relation to our own political cultural context. But we have also been formed by the context of the Sweden of the 1970s and 1980s, where new social movements have had difficulty establishing their own identities, where the institutionalized hold of the old movements of the working class continues to exercise a strong degree of hegemony over political and social life. Most of all, our transatlantic context provides us with the kind of distance necessary for recombination.

At the personal level, our understanding of social movements is based on involvement and the ambition to play the role of the "partisan" theorist. In the United States, we played the role as students, learning theory in order to be able to contribute to the movement, and in Sweden, we have tried to play the role as public intellectuals, theorizing with environmentalists and other activists both in and out of movements. In spite of rumors to the contrary (for instance, Jacoby 1987), public intellectuals are not a dying breed; indeed, as we will show in the pages that follow, out of the new social movements of the past 20 years has emerged a whole set of new intellectual activities and indeed a new generation of professional intellectuals. It is our hope that this book will provide at least some evidence for the positive contribution which social movements make to the development of knowledge.

Contributions to our own development have come from many

quarters. Particularly important for this book has been the support of the Swedish Research Council for the Humanities and Social Sciences for our project on "Environmentalism and Knowledge." We would like to thank the council, and its sociology committee, for giving us the opportunity to develop our approach to social movements. At an earlier stage in the project, we worked in cooperation with Jacqueline Cramer and Jeppe Laessoe in a comparative study of environmental movements in Sweden, Denmark, and the Netherlands, and would like to thank them for their active involvement in developing the terminology that we explicate in the following pages. For reviewing chapters and encouraging us to think more clearly, we would like to thank Arni Sverrisson, Chris Rootes, Aant Elzinga, Johanna Esseveld, and Jeff Alexander, and, of course, Tony Giddens, who gave us more comments than we felt we needed when we thought we had reached the end. We would like to thank Tony for the support of a publisher and a colleague. And for our wives and daughters – our own little movements – we simply ask forgiveness for all the times when our minds were off in the theoretical clouds far away from the cognitive praxis that makes up family life.

# 1

# Social movements and sociology

In the chilly atmosphere of the cold war, sociologists in Europe and the United States were rediscovering social movements, a social phenomenon that had once been central to the discipline. Although the immediate context of this rediscovery was the polarized world of the "totalitarian" East and the "free" West, its roots lie deeper in the past. In the 1930s the fascist and communist movements had upset the political order in Germany and Italy and had appeared to threaten the very basis of democratic society. Some of the scholars who were responsible for the rediscovery of social movements were themselves the victims of this political turmoil, and their conceptualizations reflected this experience. Thus, Rudolf Heberle, a political refugee from Nazi Germany, published one of the first textbooks devoted entirely to the subject, *Social Movements: An Introduction to Political Sociology*, while professor of sociology at Louisiana State University in the United States (Heberle 1951). Heberle's book is typical of the postwar period in that it concentrates on the importance of ideology (communist and fascist) in the formation of social movements, on why individuals might want to participate in them, and ends with a warning about the threat such movements represent to democratic political systems like that of the United States.

Social movements were conceptualized as potentially dangerous forms of noninstitutionalized collective political behavior, which, if left unattended, threatened the stability of established ways of life. It was thus important for sociologists and citizens alike to gain knowledge of such movements and be able to make rational judgments about their potential danger to established society. While hardened in the 1950s, this way of conceiving social movements, as relatively spontaneous forms of collective action, had its roots in the 1930s and the unsettling events that accompanied the collapse of the world industrial economy.

## Social movements as collective behavior

In 1934, one year after Adolf Hitler came to power in Germany at the head of a mass movement, the American sociologist Herbert Blumer published an "Outline of collective behavior" (Evans 1969) in which he provided criteria for studying the formation of new forms of collective identity and for classifying crowd behavior. In the political context of the rise of European fascism, building upon a scientific interest in the effects of industrialization and urbanization on individual attitudes and beliefs, Blumer outlined a new way of conceptualizing social movements as a form of collective behavior. While many contemporary American social scientists viewed collective behavior in negative terms, with associations not only to what was occurring in Europe, but also to the emotionalism to be found in crowds, Blumer pointed to some positive aspects. He indicated the potential social creativity in the new forms of "symbolic interaction" that might accompany the breaking of the routines of normal, institutionalized behavior.

Blumer's symbolic interactionist perspective called attention to the emergence of new norms in the "adaptive behavior," the problem-solving and learning orientation, potentially present in spontaneous collective behavior. His individual-oriented, social psychological focus was to form one central strand in the sociological study of social movements, and was adapted and developed in the coming decades and later systematized in the work of Ralph Turner and Lewis Killian (1957). A second strand, which was formed in the same political context and disciplinary framework, took shape around the structure-oriented functionalism of Talcott Parsons.

In 1942 Talcott Parsons wrote an essay entitled "Sociological aspects of fascist movements" in which he sought to explain to the English-speaking world the rational basis of the apparently irrational events taking place in Europe and the Far East (Parsons 1969). In attempting to explain fascist movements in order to make political judgments about them, Parsons drew on the classical social theory of Max Weber and Emile Durkheim. About fascism as a social movement, Parsons wrote:

> This process [rationalization], looked at from the point of view of its dynamic impact on the social system, rather than the absolute significance of rationalistic patterns, has an uneven incidence on the different elements in the social structure. In the first place, it tends to divide elements of the population according to whether they tend toward what are, in rationalistic terms, the more "progressive" or "emancipated" values or patterns of conduct, or the more conservative "backward" or traditional patterns. This introduces a basis of fundamental structuring in the differentiation of attitudes. It is a basis which also tends to coincide with other bases of strain in the structuring of interests ... (p. 77)

As these thoughts were further developed into what was to become the "structural-functionalist" perspective, the emergence of a social movement was explained in terms of "strains" related to the uneven development within the various systems of action that make up a social system or a differentiated modern society. Thus fascism resulted from the tensions inherent in modernization, in the uneven effects of industrialization, democratization, and cultural change on various social groups. From this perspective, individuals were both differently affected by these larger social changes occurring "behind their backs," and forced to take sides. From this societal point of view, individual involvement and social movements themselves could be judged as progressive or reactionary, on the basis of their stance toward modernization. As with Heberle, modernization is here identified with westernization, with the establishment of political institutions and traditions similar to those in the United States or England.

While substantially different on many counts and the source of both personal and professional antagonisms, the views of Blumer and Parsons nonetheless had enough in common to form together what has come to be called the collective behavior approach to the study of social movements. Built around a synthesis of sociological and psychological theories, with a competitive yet seemingly acceptable division of labor between the macro-oriented structural functionalist and the micro-oriented symbolic interactionists, the collective behavior perspective was to dominate the study of social movements until the late 1960s.[1]

Besides the common political and scientific interests, the basic insight upon which this conceptualization grew was that individuals acted differently when they formed into spontaneous groups, an insight which can be traced, especially in the case of Parsons and structural-functionalism, to theories of crowd behavior and mass psychosis developed by Gustave LeBon at the end of the nineteenth century and Sigmund Freud at the beginning of the twentieth (see LeBon 1960; Freud 1945). The basic idea propounded here was that spontaneous gatherings of individuals serve as the basis for an emergent collective identity which cannot be explained merely with its individual members. Differences concerned the interpretation of this fact, that is whether it should be viewed positively as adaptive behavior or negatively as irrational or deviant behavior, and how it was to be explained, in terms of changes in individual attitudes and beliefs or in terms of structural strains.

As the collective behavior perspective developed throughout the 1950s and 1960s, these differences in interpretation solidified into different schools of thought. On the one side, those more inclined toward Blumer's symbolic interactionism tended to look for emergent norms, processes of self-regulation and internal reform, as well as spontaneous processes of social learning and creativity in collective behavior (Turner and Killian 1957); on the other, those closer to Parsons's structural-functionalism looked for the societal determinants of collective behavior, the social "strains" which conditioned their formation.

In a similarly innovative manner to Turner and Killian's summation of the symbolic interactionist side, Smelser's *Theory of Collective Behaviour* (1962) brought the structural-functionalist position regarding social movements to a creative conclusion. Following the path laid out by Parsons, Smelser rooted the emergence of collective behavior in spontaneous responses to structural strains in society. This macro orientation also focused attention on the political system in which collective behavior emerged. Thus, Smelser discussed the "structural conduciveness," the general social conditions, which direct collective behavior along determined paths.

Like the symbolic interactionists, Smelser was concerned with the changing beliefs that accompanied collective behavior. However, his more functionalist orientation focused on the imposition of generalized beliefs, the role of ideologies and of leaders in crystallizing vaguely felt complaints and directing collective action. Thus, where Turner and Killian developed Blumer's approach in focusing on the effects of collective behavior on individual participants and on the processes of collective will and identity formation in social movements, Smelser followed Parsons in focusing on the structural contexts in which collective behavior took place. To this end, Smelser clarified the structural-functional approach to social movements by identifying six conditions which affect their emergence and development: *structural conduciveness*, the pecularities of a particular society create different opportunities and avenues for protest; *structural strains*, the actual underlying causes of complaint; *generalized beliefs*, the role of ideologies and ideologists in shaping the way protest and complaint is understood by actors; *precipitating factors*, the specific sparks that ignite protest, *leadership and communication*, to direct and coordinate; and, finally, *the operation of social control*, the way established authorities react.

Despite differences in levels of analysis and aspirations concerning theory construction and explanation, a set of common assumptions, including the political interests mentioned earlier, united the collective behaviorist approach. Jean Cohen (1985) has succinctly summarized these assumptions in the following way, (pp. 671–2)

> (1) There are two distinct kinds of action: institutional-coventional and noninstitutional-collective behaviour. (2) Non-institutional-collective behaviour is action that is not guided by existing social norms but is formed to meet undefined or unstructured situations. (3) These situations are understood in terms of a breakdown either in the organs of social control or in the adequacy of normative integration, due to structural changes. (4) The resulting strains, discontent, frustration, and aggression lead the individual to participate in collective behaviour. (5) Noninstitutional-collective behaviour follows a "life cycle", open to causal analysis, which moves from spontaneous crowd action to the formation of publics and social movements. (6) The emergence and growth of movements within this cycle occurs through crude processes of communication: contagion, rumour, circular reaction, diffusion, etc.

These common assumptions have been the starting point for almost all contemporary discussions of social movements, particularly in the United States. While most sociologists have attempted to move beyond this earlier dominant perspective, it has proved difficult to develop an alternative conceptualization of similar explanatory power. Our own attempt in this volume to expound a cognitive approach to social movements is also indebted in many ways to the collective behavior tradition, but, by linking explicitly to alternative European sociological traditions, departs from both its political and scientific assumptions.

## Social democracy: movement as institution

While the collective behavior approach was taking form in the United States, partly, as we have argued, in interpretive response to events in Europe, other traditions were at work in the latter. The more class and tradition bound European societies produced their own ways of understanding social movements, as well as their own strategies for dealing with them. Two aspects affecting this interpretation stand out: on the one hand, the linkage between social scientific conceptualization and politics was much more apparent than in the United States; and on the other, the accounts of collective phenomena, such as social movements, tended to be more consciously interpreted in light of established theoretical traditions.

Collective behaviorists in the United States sought to conceptualize social movements as observable empirical phenomena developing according to their own inner logic, which the social scientist could classify according to agreed-upon criteria of empirical observation. The more philosophically informed European sociologists tended to conceptualize social movements as theoretically constituted objects, in which political judgment as well as theoretical tradition played a central role.[2] The two main competing theoretical-political interpretations were, not surprisingly, those of Marx and Weber.

Like his later followers in the United States, Weber tended to view crowds and masses with trepidation rather than expectation. They were seen as aspects of social transition, perhaps necessary, but at best temporary. His studies of charismatic authority and styles of leadership point more to the dangers of collective behavior than to any positive potential (Weber 1978: 241ff. and 1376–7). Regarding the labor movement, Weber preferred the "mature" politics of organized trade unions and political parties to the mass politics of social movements (Mommsen and Osterhammel 1987).[3] Given the individual orientation and rationalist model of action which underlies Weber's approach as a whole, it should not be surprising that terms like "alienated," "romantic," and "value-oriented," are common in discussions of social movements which take their inspiration from Weber. Even where the attempt is primarily focused on drawing out the rationality underlying apparently nonrational actions, the Weberian concern with values lives on (Rootes 1978).

On the other hand, Weber's studies of bureaucracy, and that of his friend and confidant Robert Michels on German social democracy (Michels 1959), have influenced the study of social movements (in both Europe and America) in yet another direction. Strong emphasis is placed on the role organization and leadership play in affecting the effectiveness of social movements as strategic actors. Focusing on the relations between types of leadership and forms of organizations, Michels argued that the routinization of charismatic leadership flowed from the establishment of bureaucratic structures. Both were seen as necessary aspects of the maturation of social movements in modern society, by which dynamic social forces were transformed into stagnant, top-heavy institutions, where an oligarchy of pragmatic "petty bourgeois" leaders concerned themselves more with reproducing their own power than with changing society. This particular outcome of the institutionalization of mass movements has come to be called the "Weber-Michels model" (see Zald and McCarthy 1987). The argument that it is unavoidable and necessary has stirred sufficient debate to have led to the construction of an alternative "resource mobilization" approach to the study of social movements. This will be discussed in more detail below.[4]

Marxists have tended to view social movements with expectation and anticipation, signs of an impending collapse of an existing (repressive) capitalist order and as the potential source of its replacement by socialism. Movements, for Marxists, were thus taken as collective expressions of discontent and potential bases for social change (Eyerman 1984). The model of the collective actor here was that of the "self-activating class" rather than the faceless mass. The issue is not so much why social movements emerge and or how they take form, but rather what they represent in terms of their social basis, their class composition. This, in turn, is related to their political potential, whether or not they represent progressive or retrogressive forces, as well as to the quality of the challenge they raise to the existing order. What mass movements require, for Marxists, is not so much explanation as evaluation and mediation, judgments about their potential for progressive and fundamental social change and about the possibilities for influencing them in those directions. Terms like "progressive," "defensive," "single-issue," "radical," etc., are common in Marxist discussions of social movements.[5]

These theoretical-political differences were strongest in the early part of the twentieth century, when the tensions associated with the development of modern society were most strongly felt. They emerged again in the late 1920s and early 1930s in the turmoil associated with the collapse of industrial economies and the social and political polarization which eventually culminated in the rise of fascism and the beginning of the Second World War. They were mollified when a reformist social democracy solidified its hegemony over the European labor movements, and most especially after the Second World War, when a new political consensus was established around the "welfare state," in which various social democratic parties were given a central role. The conflict between labor and capital, which both Marxists and Weberians agreed to be the most fundamental of modern society, appeared to be successfully institutionalized. Social movements had moved from the noninstitutionalized margins of society to its very core.

While the expansion of the state as a central coordinating mechanism in society took place in both Europe and America, there was a fundamental difference in the character and relative strength of the social forces which stimulated this state expansion. This differences directly affected the way social movements were conceptualized by sociologists. The existence of a strong, institutionalized, reformist social democratic labor movement in all the countries of Western Europe affected the way social movements were conceived by social scientists and, perhaps more importantly, the very possibility for "new" social movements to take form. In fact, differences in the strength and character of national labor movements and social democratic parties help explain not only national differences in sociological interest but also differences in the strength of new social movements themselves (Jamison et al., 1990).

Sweden, where social democracy has been at its strongest, provides an instructive example. As modified by the interaction between a centralized and hierarchically organized labor movement and a powerful and reformist social democratic political party, the very term "movement" (*rörelse*) came to be identified with labor and the working class as such. Thus the collective behaviorist definition of social movements as a form of noninstitutionized behavior found no place in Swedish social science. As the discipline itself was from its origins closely connected to what has been characterized as the "social democratic image of society" (Castles 1978), all "progressive" social change was identified with and said only to occur through the institutionalized "movement."

Where social democractic ideas greatly inform a political culture, social movements tend to be conceptualized either as an institutionalized form of collective behavior, or, when investigated in its early stages, as preinstitutionalized forms of conflict. Within this context, focus is placed upon mobilization, either as internal processes set in motion and orchestrated from above, or as external challenges to be siphoned into the established channels. The starting point of analysis is the institution, the established networks of a well-organized society, not the individual, the crowd, or structurally rooted strains.

In the United States where social democracy is weak and where the labor movement is aggressively anti-ideological, the explicitly political distinction between movements and institutions, so common in Europe, was conceptualized as a distinction between values and norms. For example, Smelser (1962) distinguished general movements from social movements, and in reference to the latter, value oriented from norm oriented social movements. General movements were identified as long-term drifts or shifts in societal norms and values, gradual changes in attitude and consciousness which led to changes in behavior – examples here were those of the relations between men and women, changing roles at home and at work – while social movements were identified as those more immediately observable, more or less coherent outbursts of collective behavior, which emerged now and then to push these long-term changes along. Thus, a social movement was the observable expression of general movements, of long-term shifts in attitude and belief.

As in the social democratic views discussed above, structural functionalism subscribes to an evolutionary theory of social change. Where the one sees society becoming more rational as the concerns of movements are institutionalized, the other sees social movements as noninstitutionalized, yet rational and instrumental, forms of collective behavior, and thereby as more or less necessary phases in long-term processes of social change. Change, as expressed through social movements, was described as occurring through a series of stages: conflict and confrontation, inclusion and institutionalization, new conflict and collective behavior. As with many European theorists, the main mechanism of inclusion for Smelser was the state, with the professional social scientist given the role of the expert who, as in Weber's formulation, mediates between the general society and the politician.

## The 1960s and the "new social movements"

The student movements came as a shock to sociologists. Neither branch of the collective behavior approach, the established Marxian or Weberian theories of social change gave any prediction of the range and force of the conflicts that rocked Western Europe and the United States in the late 1960s. In France, a coalition of student and worker demonstrations and occupations brought the country to a standstill and the government to crisis. In the United States, demonstrations, strikes and occupations became an almost everyday occurrence, as students, in part inspired by events in France and other parts of the world, began to think of themselves as the main bearers of social change in modern society.[6]

None of this found easy explanation in the existing schools of thought. With its macro orientation focusing on strain and social deviance, the structural-functionalist collective behaviorism had difficulty accounting for social conflict in the university, one of the most integral modern institutions, led by the most adjusted of social groups, university students. These students after all were the elite of modern society on their way to professional careers as the next generation of leaders. They were neither deviants on the margins of society nor were they outcasts at the cutting edge of structural strain. Their movement could not be explained according to structural functionalism.

The more individual oriented symbolic interactionists faced a similar difficulty: how to explain why apparently well-adjusted students could be attracted to beliefs and forms of political behavior which would obviously threaten their careers. Even if one rejected the more rationalistic theories of motivation, symbolic interactionists concerned with social movements could not easily account for the great enthusiasm shown by university students for revolutionary ideas and disruptive behavior. New concepts and interpretations were necessary.

For their part, the dominant marxist approaches which focused on relations of production and the conflict between labor and capitial were not in a position to explain student revolutionaries, except as alienated members of the middle class. For orthodox Marxists, only when conflict involved issues of production and directly engaged the working class could one speak of a real social movement. At best, student conflicts could be the spark that ignited the "progressive" forces for social change in society, and students, like those *déclassés* "intellectuals" who participated in the working-class movements of the nineteenth century, could be part of the vanguard of revolutionary social change. Thus neither the actors nor the movements were considered in their own terms but only in relation to other groups and conflicts. Explanation from this point of view would have to appeal to "secondary contradictions" or to contradictory class locations, with the underlying political interest of linking these actors to others who were seen as more critically located in the constitution of society. These were points of view which united orthodox Marxists and structural functionalists.

Thus the early accounts of the student movements had difficulty taking them seriously. Social scientists often found it congenial to rest on psychological explanation, focusing, even if in a sympathetic way, on the "alienation of youth" (Keniston 1965), on the conflict of generations (Feuer 1969), and, even where they offered more sociological analysis, on personal frustration and status inconsistency (Lipset 1967). For the most part, student movements were considered part of a new generation struggling for recognition, and thus in need of striking out against their elders and "the establishment" who were withholding such recognition.[7] Only a few authors, however, such as Keniston (1968), saw this in a positive light. In other forms of explanation which sought to combine the psychological with the structural, students were said to represent a new generation with "higher" needs, who, precisely because they were raised in middle-class comfort, were in a position to seek "postmaterial" values, concerning one's relation to self-fulfillment and to more altruistic goals connected to the quality of life (Maslow 1962, 1964).

Caught in the constraints of the established perspectives, social scientists had difficulty seeing more in the student revolts than the frustrated rebellion of the privileged, or, like the popular press, the misguided victims of outside agitators and ideologies. There was, of course, some truth to be found in these accounts. Most of those involved were indeed young. The category "youth" was in the process of being given new meaning in the early 1960s. Commercially, being young was becoming grounds for a distinct style of life, with clothing, music, and film to match. Socially, youth subcultures were emerging in which new relations between the sexes were being experimented with. In addition, being young seemed to involve greater numbers and to last for a longer period of time than ever before. The young thus seemed to be forming a distinct political and social group.

Disgruntled structural functionalists, like Lipset, were on the right track, however, when they pointed to possible strains within the systems of higher education in the industrialized societies: something was happening in higher education that could be the grounds for the frustration of the young. Higher education, especially in the United States but also in Western Europe, was undergoing a change: a "massification" was taking place and a knowledge industry being established, as a more qualified workforce was required to man the high-tech industries projected for the coming decades (Kerr 1966). Looking at this new movement (which actually was several movements at once) as the revolt of the privileged however was to miss the point: this was not a struggle to regain or retain privilege, at least not at first or solely, but rather an attempt to question and redirect wider processes of social change by a new group of actors in the process of forming a collective identity.

Being a movement dominated by actors engaged primarily in intellectual pursuits, it should thus not be surprising that student activists began to develop their own theoretical understandings of the movements. In the US the first such internal accounts focused on the revolt of intellectuals against what was loosely formulated as the knowledge society and its central institution, the university. In Europe, where the left–right political divide was more strongly felt, neomarxist explanations quickly surfaced. These, along with the notion of a "new left," were imported to the US and spread through the mass media.

Influenced by left-wing traditions, movement intellectuals formulated theories which attempted to link the movement to other social groups and to wider societal processes: the theory of the new working class (Mallet 1976), new strategies for labor (Gorz 1967) were formulations of a type of social theory which lived in a newly constituted world between established scholarly institutions and disciplines and the political practice of social movements. Like the student movement itself these theories mediated between the abstract world of scholarship and the practical world of politics.

Sociology began to feel the influence of these intellectual currents and the movement, since its conceptualizations of society were at the heart of the struggle and many activists turned to the field. Marx was readmitted to the pantheon of the founding fathers of the discipline and other forms of marxism were rediscovered and reinvented. Wilhelm Reich's studies of the link between sexual revolution and social revolution (Reich 1972) and Critical Theory's similarly radical syntheses of Marx and Freud can be considered examples of this process of "recollection" (Marcuse 1964, 1969). All this helped stimulate new approaches to the study of society and within that to social movements themselves.

Because of the nature of the subject, the study of social movements was one of the sub-areas of sociology most affected by the student movement. As noted, many activists were social science students and many faculty members in these disciplines actively supported them. The study of social change, including that of revolution, and social movements became in the process topics of key interest. The new impetus provided by the student movement and the rediscovery of critical and alternative traditions latent within the discipline combined with the new activist role of the sociologist to challenge the then dominant modes of conceptualizing social movements. New approaches involved not only interpreting the contemporary social movements, but also reinterpreting older ones within the new frameworks. In a sense, our cognitive approach is the second generation of this process of reinterpretation.

The first generation was more connected to an activist role in the student movements themselves, more connected in other words to the cognitive praxis of the movement. This new conceptualization was formulated in the pamphlets, journals, and newsletters which were either directly or indirectly connected to movement organizations, or by those who thought of themselves in that way. From the pamphlets and workshops of the early Students for a Democratic Society to the more academic *New Left Notes* and *New Left Review*, movement intellectuals laid the foundation and attempted to influence the theoretical self-understanding of the student movements. This created an alternative to the established academic discourse on social movements, a discourse which, in turn, impacted upon the established discourses and their conceptualizations of social movements.

In Europe, where another set of political ideologies and social scientific conceptualizations held away, a different kind of development was taking place in the wake of the student movements. A wave of extraparliamentary political activity was being conceptualized as "new" social movements: the women's, peace, and environmentalist movements. Rooted in a normative theory of society, the term "new social movements" was designed to make a clear separation between these movements and the institutionalized "old" movements of the working class. In addition, the distinction referred to fundamental shifts in social structure, the emergence of "postindustrial" society (Touraine 1981; Offe 1985; Melucci 1985). Thus the terms "new" and "old" were meant to have more than a temporal reference. Postindustrial movements, it was argued, engage different actors, different loci of conflict and different issues than those of industrial society. Even if on the empirical level, these "new" social movements exhibited characteristics and even ideas which recalled the early, preinstitutional days of the "old" labor movement, it was necessary, because of the postulated shifts in social formation, to speak of new movements and to move beyond the existing frameworks of explanation. From this point of view, Marxist and Weberian approaches to social movements were seen as being too strongly rooted in an industrial capitalist society to provide categories which could be applied to contemporary conflicts. Similarly, collective behaviorism was limited by its origins in the problems and conflicts of postwar American society – and American social science (Melucci 1989). In addition, because of its tendency to treat all social movements in the same way, as following similar patterns of development and so on, collective behaviorism missed the real historical significance of the new social movements.

## Resource mobilization

In the post-1960s academy in the United States, the collective behavior approach was being challenged by what has come to be known as the resource mobilization approach (Zald and McCarthy 1987). As opposed to collective behaviorism, resource mobilization takes its starting point for analysis in organizations and not in the individual. Thus it does not center around the question of why individuals join social movements, the rationality or irrationality of their intentions or behavior as participants, but rather on the effectiveness with which movements, that is movement organizations, use the resources in attempting to achieve their goals. Here the prime research question is not who the actors are or what motivates them, or what wider historical or structural meaning a particular movement may have, but rather why some movements are more successful than others. Success here is defined as a function of how clearly orgainzational goals are defined and how effectively its available resources – people, material, and ideas – are put to use both in mobilizing support and in seeing to it that the established institutions take seriously the aims expressed by the movement.

From the perspective of resource mobilization the collective behavior approach remains locked in an individual-oriented social psychological problematic on the one side, and into an abstract structural-functionalist "grand theory" on the other. To really understand social movements, it was argued, one needed a middle-range approach like that provided by organizational analysis. While not directly the outgrowth of the student movement, resource mobilization reflects the dissatisfaction with the collective behaviorist approach that was connected to the latter's response to that movement, both personally and sociologically. Thus, the rejection of collective behaviorism by a new generation of sociologists concerned with social movements and the search for alternative modes of analysis, of which resource mobilization was one, can be understood as a challenging of established sociology. Just as rejecting "the establishment" in all its guises was one of the central rhetorical themes that united the various student movements, so rejecting "mainstream" sociology was important in the formation of a new generation of sociologists. Even if they were not themselves activists, the new generation of sociologists concerned with social movements was deeply affected by the student movement, and this in turn has affected their conceptualization of social movements.

### Recent debates

As noted, the most widely discussed terminological package in the current debates about social movements, sometimes given the status of a paradigm, is resource mobilization. Central here is the distinction between movements and movement organizations, and the attempt to identify for every social movement a particular social movement sector (Garner and Zald 1985), sometimes called industry, within which the various organizations coexist. Focusing on the "rationality" of social movements, resource mobilization studies the mechanisms through which movements recruit their members and the organizational forms through which mobilization of both human and social resources takes place. The key notion of "resources" is broadly defined to include not only the classic land, labor, and capital but also authority, social status, and personal initiative. Its proponents are mostly concerned with the interaction between activists, that is, individual movement actors and the movement organizations. Through what institutional channels does an individual become a member of a movement? How is the human capital embodied in an individual accumulated in a social movement, and used most efficiently?

A second important approach that has developed in recent years, which sometimes is portrayed as a branch of resource mobilization (Jenkins 1989), focuses on the personal motivations that lead to participation in social movements. Sharing a social psychological interest with the older collective behavior approach, these more individually oriented sociologists and social historians, led by the American sociologist Charles Tilly, have provided a number of studies of particular movements or of individuals within movements. Often documenting their findings with meticulous detail and extensive interviews, this "particularist" school of social movement research investigates social movements as vehicles for a political socialization process. What influence does a social movement have on a particular individual's political activity? What was it in an individual's background or upbringing – in her socalled social network – that leads to her getting involved in a particular movement?

Tilly defines the collective action typical of social movements in terms of the pursuit of common interests (Tilly 1978), and is concerned primarily with the effectiveness of tactical decision-making. In describing this effectiveness, Tilly discusses social movements as moving from "organization to mobilization" of resources around shared interests and, finally, to the realization of effective action in specific opportunity structures. Since the opportunity for collective action varies with historical and cultural circumstances, Tilly adds the dimension of historical context to his study of social movements.

A common concern which links the particularists and the more formalistic resource mobilization approach is explaining the sacrifices made by individual actors. In their common challenge to collective behaviorism, both emphasize the rationality of human action: actors are assumed to calculate the costs and benefits of participation in any action. An immediate problem of accounting for participation in the generally risky business of political protest emerges. If rational calculation alone is considered, actors might likely choose to be "free-riders" (Olson 1965), letting others take the risks while hoping to still reap the benefits themselves. A theory of social networks, which focuses on the "pull" of social pressure as a form of "solidarity" is used to provide an explanation of why calculating actors might choose to engage in behavior they might otherwise seek to avoid (Tilly 1985).

As was previously the case in many areas of social analysis, here too a gulf has emerged between American and European sociologists in the understanding of social movements. While most American sociologists tend to fall into one of the above two categories, in Europe the most common approach has been to analyze social movements as carriers of political projects, as historical actors. The French sociologist Alain Touraine (1981, 1983) has, in a series of books, investigated the "new social movements" as potential bearers of new social interests, and the German social philosopher Jürgen Habermas (1987b) has speculated on the potential civilizational role of the new movements. Many of those who have investigated the new environmental and peace movements in Europe have looked at them from this more "external" perspective, not as mobilizers of resources to achieve certain ends but as transforming agents of political life. Looked at as new social movements many European sociologists attempt to place them into a broader historical context, thus constituting a third approach to the study of social movements. Here social movements are described as the dominant social forces of a postindustrial society and more internal questions of actor motivation and resource mobilization tend to be disregarded.

Central to Touraine's approach, as it is to ours, is the process of collective will formation, the ways through which movements come to recognize themselves as collective actors with a historical project. For Touraine, this process involves an interaction around three interconnected poles – totality, identity, and opposition – and the identity of a social movement takes shape in the totality of a social field of action in opposition to an historical Other (Touraine 1981: 81).

The key concept of historicity has a double meaning in Touraine's approach to social movements. It refers on the one hand to a distinct stage of historical development, the "self-programmed society," where societies are said to have reached a level at which self-reflection upon the foundations of social life becomes possible, what classical sociologists identified as modernity. On the other hand, Touraine's notion of historicity gives special place to social movements in actualizing this universal process of social reflexivity. For Touraine a social movement, as distinct from a protest organization or mobilization campaign, is characterized by the realization of historicity, by the self-conscious awareness that the very foundations of society are at stake or in contest.

The aim of his empirical studies of contemporary social protest has been to show the validity of this distinction, and to develop a method of action research to overcome the gap between the narrowly defined aims of activists and the wider claims of historicity. In addition to the underlying theory of historical development, where "in post-industrial society, social movements form around what is called consumption in the name of personal or collective identity . . . not in relation to the system of ownership" (Touraine 1977: 323), his distinctly politically motivated, normative approach clearly separates Touraine from the pragmatic resource mobilization approach and from the more historically informed particularists.

We are not the first to recognize the incommensurability of these different approaches. In an important article already mentioned in our discussion of collective behaviorism, Jean Cohen (1985) suggested that what was at issue was a difference of emphasis. Where the Americans concerned with social movements tended to focus on the instrumentality of movement strategy formation, that is, on how movement organizations went about trying to achieve their goals, the Europeans focused on identity formation, on how movements produced new historical identities for society. Borrowing from Habermas, she urged the development of a synthetic approach by which movements could be analyzed as both instrumental and communicative, as both resource mobilizers and resource generators. While Cohen's synthesis remains attractive at the level of theory, it fails to address the substantial methodological and contextual difficulties that stand in the way of its realization in research practice. A mere combination of approaches would lead to a loss of the particular contributions that each approach has provided to the understanding of social movements. What would be gained in grand theory would be lost in empirical research.

A more recent and fruitful attempt to bridge this gap in under-standing is provided by Klandermans and Tarrow (in Klandermans et al., 1988). Here the emphasis, like ours in a recent volume on the new environmentalism (Jamison et al., 1990), is on compar-ative analysis. The claim is made that European and American approaches to social movements suffer from different biases. The Americans, it is here suggested, are interested in the mechanisms by which movements recruit participants, that is, resource mobiliza-tion, while the Europeans are interested in studying how social problems are transformed into social movements, that is, identify-ing mobilization potentials.[8] Klandermans and Tarrow propose a synthesis between American and European approaches by trying to find a common ground. The synthesis proposed seeks to combine resource mobilization with the interest in political opportunity structures that is popular among Europeans. It is, we would sug-gest, thus a kind of reduction to a middle level, where mobilization becomes a common denominator that can link the interests of the two schools. More specifically, Klandermans and Tarrow suggest that the processes of what they call consensus mobilization are a blind spot and thus a meeting ground for both approaches: how movements "attempt to influence the perceptions of potential parti-cipants." By a terminological sleight of hand, incommensurability has been replaced by a new Mertonian-style theory of the middle range. But it remains to be seen whether this synthesis can provide any more comprehensive understanding than can Cohen's.

What is missing, we feel, from both of these attempted syntheses is a contextual diagnosis of the incompatibilities of the various approaches. It is no accident, nor is it merely a function of geo-graphy that social movement sociologists approach their subject in different ways. Rather, it is due to a number of interrelated histor-ical and cultural factors, derived from both the external and inter-nal intellectual contexts within which sociological schools are formed. More specifically, the incompatibilities of approaches de-rive from different political cultures, especially the different roles played by social movements in the political formation of the societies. These roles have also led to different meanings being given to the notion of movement and of social movement in the different political discourses. A second, more internal set of con-textual factors are the different intellectual traditions, including as central aspects philosophies of history and theories of knowledge which have affected the ways in which sociology has been practiced and social movements have been conceptualized. Finally, and perhaps most importantly, the different sociological approaches are based on different personal relations of the sociologist to the social movements being investigated. The nature and degree of empathy/ animosity that the sociologist brings to his/her investigation is an important element often neglected by sociologists in their diagnoses of difference. But it is, we suggest, a significant formative influence that crosscuts the geographical differences, and can be found on both sides of the Atlantic.

In the rest of this chapter, we will examine each of these contextual elements in the process of developing a comprehensive framework for understanding and analyzing social movements. This is central to our approach. For us, sociology cannot easily be disembodied from the sociologists who practice it. And thus the contexts, individual, institutional, and historical, through which the sociologist has been constituted are also constitutive of the sociology that she produces.

By better understanding the sources of the tensions between the dominant schools of thought, the reader will thus be in a better position to grasp our own approach to reading social movements. This reading is based on a new set of concepts that reconnect to earlier traditions in the sociology of knowledge and the philosophy of history and to a reflexive mode of sociohistorical analysis that has been neglected in most of the recent discussions of social movements. Of central importance are the related concepts of knowledge interest and cognitive praxis which we have utilized in earlier work to capture and critically reflect upon the core identity and developmental trajectories of the new environmental movements of the 1970s and 1980s. As with our other key concept, movement intellectual, knowledge interest is both an analytical and a critical tool in our approach. It is used both to grasp the historical meaning of a social movement and to evaluate its political potential and impact. We will return in later chapters to a more detailed discussion of these concepts. In particular, we will apply them to other social movements, both in other parts of the world as well as in other historical periods.

## The intellectual context

An appropriate starting point for understanding the differences among the approaches to social movements is the recognition that the three dominant schools are rooted in different intellectual traditions. This is why they concern themselves with different "levels" of social movement praxis. The particularists, focusing as they do on individual motivation and socialization, are concerned with an "actor" level, where social movements are seen as collections of individuals and where interest is focused on individual actions and reactions. The resource mobilization school focuses on a group level of organizations and collectivities, where social mechanisms of inclusion and exclusion form the central focus of analysis and where individuals are treated as types, depersonalized units in decision-making models. The new social movement theorists are concerned with a macrostructural level of society, where movements are seen as historical actors articulating long-term trends and deepseated social forces.

The particularists are rooted in an individual oriented tradition of social thought which starts from the assumption that society is constituted by autonomous actors. These actors are seen as entering into collectivities of their own free will; society is conceptualized as the creation of voluntary involvement in collectivities. There is here no abstract social interest outside of the individual, and individuals participate in society only to the extent that their individuality is served. The underlying social ontology could thus be termed atomistic, and the tradition's social philosophy has grown out of the Hobbesian-Lockean concern with individual freedom and personal autonomy.

In sociology this tradition has been formed primarily through the Weberian concern with the motivations of individual actors and their value orientations, as touched upon earlier. Knowledge of society is gained by uncovering the frameworks through which actors interpret the world and their own place in it. Social change is explained through the changes in frameworks, the changes in values that determine the actions of individuals. Thus Weber (1958) explained the development of capitalism in terms of a change in the worldview or ethical orientation of the capitalist, and Smelser (1962) explained the rise of modern industrial society in terms of the structures of motivation that guide the actions of the participants in the process. In both cases, social processes are seen as resulting from value transformation. And it is the categorization of those value transformations into typologies that provides the sociologist with an understanding of the process itself. By characterizing sets of values or ideal typical variations, sociologists explain social change as primarily attitudinal or mental change.

As such, the particularist tradition in social movement research tends toward biography or collective biography, and thus the meaning of movement is perceived and interpreted through individual personal experience and recollection. With Smelser writing in the 1960s, as we earlier discussed, there was an ambition to link this value orientation to wider historical processes, for example rationalization, modernization, secularization. Smelser could thus still conceptualize social movements as both individual and collective behavior, or, as he and Parsons termed it, as both value oriented and success oriented.

In their rejection of the assumptions of collective behaviorism, the recent particularists have largely lost that ambition in their specialized search for specific explanation. Inspired by the aggressive particularism of Charles Tilly (Shorter and Tilly 1974; Tilly et al. 1975, Tilly 1978), social movements for the particularists have become largely nongeneralizable as historical phenomena. Each movement, for Tilly and his followers, has its own specific context and its own specific logic or illogic. What is crucial is the understanding of the actual individuals taking part in the movement and of the specific events that are claimed to constitute the movement. Neither suprahistorical schemes nor macrostructural processes are to be imposed onto the actual historical reality. The result is exciting historical scholarship obtained at the expense of a fragmentation of our understanding of social movements.

The resource mobilization school, on the other hand, is concerned with a "collective/organizational" level of analysis of movement organizations and organizational strategies. Where particularists look at motivations, resource mobilization looks at mechanisms and at incentives; the emphasis is not any longer on people and personal involvement and indeed stories, but on structures, strategies, and the efficient utilization and constitution of social resources. Instead of tending toward biography, resource mobilization tends toward cost/benefit analysis and economics. Where the one can thus grasp social movement praxis in all of its nonrational and very human complexity, the other simplifies a social movement to uncover its underlying rationality. The one fascinates through its individual micro-level detail, the other clarifies through its meso-level operationality.

The intellectual tradition on which resource mobilization is based comes out of the institutional approach to social development first articulated by the political economists of the eighteenth and nineteenth centuries. From Adam Smith and John Stuart Mill, a social ontology of institution formation and rational choice entered the social sciences primarily through economics. Here society is no longer seen as consisting of autonomous and for that matter interesting individuals worthy of study in their own right. Rather society is its institutions and organizational structures. Between the individual and society is posited a meso level of mediating instances, state apparatuses, corporate businesses, and institutional mechanisms. Robert Merton's (Merton 1957) theorizing at the middle range of social reality has been crucial here in opening this space to sociological analysis. More recently, the management sciences and, in particular, the theorists of industrial relations and industrial organization have been instrumental in articulating the terms of this middle-level discourse. As Alain Touraine (Touraine 1988:37) has put it, this sociology breaks with the classical notions of rationality and "speaks of a limited rationality, that is, of strategy or . . . of competition for the control of areas of uncertainty where the position of agents remains unclear. In this theory, social agents seek to maximize their interests, but they do so in an environment they control, or even know, only partially."

Rather than autonomous actors, the objects of sociological investigation are organizational agents, using a society that is not knowable in its entirety but which is manipulable. Thus social movements are seen either as the creation of entrepreneurs skillful in the manipulation or mobilization of social resources or as the playing out of social tensions and conflicts. Social change is conceptualized as conflict resolution and history is the unintended outcome of these strategic battles between organizations or "movement industries." In this perspective the motivations of actors are only interesting as they bear on economies of action. Actors, or rather agents, are seen in budgetary terms, as calculating the costs and benefits to be derived from their participation in movements. Sharing some of the individualist assumptions of the particularists, the resources mobilization school sees society as collectivities of rational actors. But where the one explores the complexity of individual motivation – indeed that is the leitmotif of the approach – the other limits attention to instrumental or rational motivations. The nonrational is by definition not important.

As mentioned, the rise of resource mobilization in the early 1970s can be seen in part as a reaction to the older collective behaviorists, symbolic interactionists as well as functionalists.

Drawing on concepts developed in political science and economics, the proponents of resource mobilization sought to interpret the social movements that were then such a visible part of the American social reality in management terms. The intellectual problem of understanding these new movements was linked to what might be termed a policy problem of containment. We will return to this confluence of sociology with the policy sciences when we discuss the context of interpretation later in the chapter.

The intellectual traditions behind the European approaches to social movements are quite different from those we have been discussing up to now. There is, of course, a common source in the classical sociologists, especially Max Weber, as we mentioned earlier. In Europe, however, Weber is drawn on more as a historian than a value sociologist, as the counterpoint to Marx in seeking explanations of historical development, indeed in characterizing historical development altogether.

Touraine in France, Habermas in Germany, Giddens in Britain give ample indication that this macrostructural sociology remains vital in European social thought. Here society is seen in terms of structures, forces, long-term processes, and projects. It is as carriers or bearers of these processes and projects that individuals and their social movements are conceptualized. Thus, much more than in America, there is a concern with distinguishing the new social movements from the old. The new social movements are located within a new historical epoch, it is argued, but there are differences as to how significant these new social movements are considered to be. We will return to thess differences when we discuss the political cultural context of social movement research in the following section.

Dieter Rucht (1988) well illustrates the different level of analysis that these European intellectual traditions inspire. Instead of mechanisms and motivations, Rucht talks, typically we feel, of themes and logics of social movements. And much of the most valuable European analysis has been at this level of understanding. The underlying ideologies and programs of social movements have been elucidated, as have the broader social and historical implications. In a book like Touraine's *The Voice and the Eye* (1981), social movements are placed in the context of a theory of history, indeed they are given the pride of place in the struggles for historicity that, for Touraine, are society.

As such, the three main approaches to social movements not only speak different languages and formulate different terminologies, they belong to different intellectual universes. Different conceptions of society and different explanatory ambitions cannot be combined easily. Nor can they enrich each other without appropriate frameworks of translation. These frameworks, as we will develop them in coming chapters, must respect the different intellectual starting points, while transcending their limited, even fragmented, contemporary manifestations. In particular, the processes of social learning, knowledge production, and intellectual creation which are dealt with by all three approaches are not encompassed within the same discourse. This, as we shall see, is because those discourses themselves have become separate and self-enclosed. A comprehensive conceptual framework must thus move forward by first returning to the sources, in particular the founders of the sociology of knowledge in the nineteenth and early twentieth centuries. Such is the task ahead.

## The political cultural context

It was the founders of the sociology of knowledge who established the now largely forgotten truth that our understanding of reality is conditioned by social historical context. The sociology of knowledge, as developed by among others Max Scheler and Karl Mannheim in the 1920s and 1930s, sought to uncover the ways in which social relations and cultural traditions influenced the development of knowledge, both in the social sciences and, for Scheler, the natural sciences as well. Recently, Therborn (1976), Gouldner (1970, 1985), Lepenies (1988), and others have applied a sociology of knowledge approach to the history of sociology and have shown some of the ways in which the classical sociologists were conditioned, in their choice of research area as well as in their conceptual framework, by the political environment in which they wrote. Elsewhere, sociologists have begun to disclose the social conditioning of the natural sciences, and there has been a revival of interest in identifying what John T. Merz at the end of the nineteenth century had labeled national styles of science, that is, the different institutional traditions and conceptual approaches that characterize scientists in particular countries (Merz 1965). As far as we know, there has been little attempt to apply these insights to the study of social movements; the difference between European and American approaches has certainly been noted and commented upon, sometimes at length, but no one has sought to ground that difference in any more fundamental contextual manner. Let us here try to indicate what such a grounding might consist of.

A first set of conditioning factors are the differences in political structure, in the ways politics are practiced in different countries. Obviously, parliamentary democracies provide different "opportunity structures" (Kitschelt 1986; Katzenstein and Mueller 1987) than a federal republic; and multiparty systems present social movements with different challenges than two-party systems. Beyond these obvious political factors are the more subtle ones, having to do with the different rule systems in different cultures, and even more importantly, with the different frameworks within which political life is conceptualized. As we have shown in our volume on the new environmentalism, there is a tradition in Denmark of alternative politics, primarily based in the countryside. That tradition was influential in the process of Danish industrialization through a network of cooperative dairies and people's high schools and it was revived in the resistance movement during the Second World War. It was largely because of such a tradition that the environmental movement was able to "mobilize" the population against nuclear energy, and it is an important reason why Danish environmentalism has merged into a broader movement of alternativism and rural collectivism. In Sweden, on the other hand, the environmental movement has been, almost from the beginning, much more parliamentary in orientation; Sweden was perhaps the only country in Western Europe where a substantial parliamentary force, the Center party, opposed nuclear energy in the early 1970s. It is thus no accident that Sweden now has the second largest green party in Europe. Where Denmark has had a tradition of extraparliamentary "movements," those in Sweden have been all but integrated into parliamentary parties. It is this kind of difference that has also affected the ways in which social movements are conceptualized in the two countries. In Denmark a movement is located on the grassroots, while in Sweden the movement merges into the party, whether it be the social democratic "movement," the farmers' "movement, " or for that matter the green "movement."

These differences in political traditions have directly influenced the study of social movements in Sweden and Denmark. Where Swedish sociology has developed a rich understanding of the social democratic "movement," Denmark has provided some of the most important studies of grassroots mobilization in some of the socalled new social movements. Where in Sweden party and movement merge into the concept of *folkrörelse* (popular movement), and such established movements are the subject of study by even state investigative commissions, in Denmark the grassroots initiatives of the alternative political culture have become a popular subject of study for sociologists, political scientists, and populist intellectuals. As touched on earlier, our point is that the different social and cultural concepts of movement have led the study of social movements into quite different directions.

It is also such differences in political culture – and in the cultural definition of social movement – that underlie the different approaches to the study of social movements in the United States, France, West Germany, and Britain. National political differences have been analyzed by Klandermans and Tarrow (1988) in relation to four core movements – student, environmental, women's, and peace. As they put it, "National traditions of social protest have firmly conditioned the 'nationalization' of the new movements of the past two decades, not because of any 'iron law' of cooptation but because the movement's need for consensus, allies, and legitimation leads them to use existing traditions of social movement organization and existing reservoirs of sentiment and expectation as raw materials" (p. 25).

Here we would like to follow their lead in pointing to national differences in political culture, especially in traditions of social movement. But we would like to take two rather fundamental further steps. On the one hand, we want to trace differences in social movement organization to long-term traditions in political culture; and secondly we want to suggest ways in which the difference in movement traditions has affected the ways sociologists study social movements. We want to supplement the stimulating remarks made by Klandermans and Tarrow with both a longer historical perspective and a sociology of knowledge analysis of social movement research.

Historically, social movements have been in the United States not merely extraparliamentary but also largely nonideological. If there has been an indigenous ideology to American social movements, it has been a homegrown populism often rooted in religion. The strong pragmatic and regional basis of social movement activity has been a recurrent feature. More recently, the social movements of the 1960s and onward have been almost aggressively single-issue oriented. From the civil rights movement to the peace movement, American activism has been characterized by issue specificity and has largely been incorporated into a tradition of public interest litigation and lobbying for legislative reform. In addition, social movements in the US have been colored by a kind of religious and moral fervor that is largely absent in Europe, where the historical struggle between the "main class antagonists" has been central for the past as well as the contemporary movements. Indeed American social movements are often, if not always, two movements in one, usually speaking different languages to different audiences and oriented toward different avenues of political change. In most movements, activist groups protesting and mobilizing at the local level develop new techniques of political opposition and usually confine their attention to one particular issue. The other "movement" consists of established organizations with lawyers and lobbyists in Washington, cut off from the grassroots but representing the interests of the public inside the halls of government. The tensions between the two movements and the gaps that often grow between them can be seen in the civil rights movement, the antiwar movement, the women's movement, the environmental movement, and the peace movement. Thus it is not surprising that the study of social movements in the United States has come to be conceptualized and practiced along two very different lines. It is as if the locally based populist tradition had inspired one school of social movement sociologists, and the organizational, public interest tradition had inspired another.

Britain is perhaps the most prominent example of a country where the conflict between capital and labor has continued to define the political culture, and thus the way social movements are conceived. It is also conspicuous in the way that the movements of the 1970s and the 1980s have largely been incorporated into the Labour party and more traditional leftist organizations. Socialist feminism, socialist environmentalism, and the various denominations of Trotskyism continue to flourish in Britain while they have largely faded away in most of the other European countries.

In France, defeat and occupation at the hands of Germany in two wars have had their effect on the poltical culture. Both nationalism and militarism are so strongly rooted that neither a substantial peace movement nor an environmental movement have been able to develop to any significant extent. The strong leftist presence has constrained the emergence of new oppositional identities; but perhaps more than in other European countries, the split between socialists and communists has fostered a sectarian attitude that has made it difficult for new alliances or constellations of movements to develop, a fact that is all the more surprising since it was in such a setting, that is, the lack of an effective opposition, that the French student movement took form in the late 1960s (Rootes 1982).

The contrast with West Germany is in this regard a striking one. There the student revolt and new leftism of the 1960s marked a clear turning point in the postwar political culture. As in the Netherlands and, to a certain extent, Austria, the 1960s represented a challenge to the dominant growth paradigm of the established political order. Here, more than elsewhere, the challenge was generational, as guilty parents saw their children go to the streets in search of a new postmaterial future. Important in the West German case is also the tinge of anti-Americanism that is found in the new movements, not surprising in a country with a continuing American military presence. In West Germany the new movements of the 1970s and 1980s have been ideologically explorative in seeking to link together the concerns of the different social movements into a unified program, and the new mobilization has also involved a reconnection to the older traditions of social movements from the pre-Nazi past. This has had an important influence not least on the ideological level. A final aspect of the West German political development has been the influence of terrorism in the 1970s and 1980s, which has affected the way that social movements are treated in certain segments of the established political culture.

This last point is also important in Italy. There a cultural tradition of charismatic and expressive politics, as well as the fascist past, have been important contextual influences on the development of social movements. Italian politics have been dominated by the class antagonism between labor and capital, and a regional split between north and south, but this antagonism has given rise to creative readjustments within the parliamentary system. As in other countries in southern Europe, the Catholic church has been an important institutional actor in Italian political life, and the spiritual coloration of politics has carried over into social movements, where the symbolic dimension plays a stronger role than perhaps anywhere else in Europe. This is reflected in how some Italian sociologists conceptualize contemporary social movements, Italian and other (Melucci 1985 and 1989).

What all this means for the study of social movements is somewhat complicated. We do not want to suggest that these differences in political culture have determined the ways in which sociologists have approached their material, but there should be no doubt that these contextual factors have affected choices in approach, explanatory strategy, and methodology. The populist, and largely nonideological, tradition of social movements in the United States has certainly encouraged voluntarist and particularistic emphases; and the emergence of resource mobilization, with its focus on mechanism rather than substance, is rooted in the American pragmatist political tradition and in the instrumental praxis and policy orientation of many social movements.

In Europe, the political context has also been a significant determinant of research orientation and emphasis. British sociologists have tended to neglect the study of social movements in recent years, and, when they do study them, they look primarily at them through the prism of the left/right dichotomy or as elements in a largely theoretical debate about social change (Banks 1972). The exception here has been Christopher Rootes's studies of the student movements (Rootes 1978, 1980, 1982) and the recent studies of the British peace movement (Taylor and Young 1987, Byrne 1988). The old categories of analysis certainly play a role in France and Germany as well, but there the impact of the new left and of the new social movements themselves has led at least some influential sociologists into speculating about long-term historical transformation. It is in France, Germany, and Italy that both the ideologists of the new movements, such as Gorz and Bahro and Alberoni, as well as the analysts of the new movements, such as Touraine and Offe, Rucht and Melucci, have been developing. Their grounding in socialist traditions has given them a different relation to the movements as well as a different conceptual framework for studying them than has been the case for their counterparts in Britain and the United States.

## The context of interpretation

It is when we look at the relations between the students of social movements and the movements they are studying that these contextual factors – both the internal or intellectual factors as well as the external or political cultural factors – become apparent. The relations between sociologist and movements, the objects of investigation, are of several types. On the one hand, there is the emotional or subjective relation, which in most cases provides one of the important reasons for studying the particular object in the first place. The kind of emotional relation can of course vary from sociologist to sociologist. And as we shall see, a good deal of the variety of approaches in social movement research can be understood in terms of different degrees of empathy/animosity. What we would stress at this point, however, is that at some level, the sociologist must identify – either positively or negatively – with her object of investigation. It is surely no accident that the study of collective behavior developed in the postwar sociologists under the influence of the Nazi and fascist movements. For the founders of collective behavior analysis, social movements represented a threat to the existing social order, an irrational form of "deviant" behavior. The identification of sociologists with their object of investigation was thus a negative one; for most American sociologists being trained in the wake of the Second World War, social movements were to be studied as manifestations of mass psychosis or hysteria.

This subjective, emotional relation to the object of investigation is transformed, in the process of investigation, into a particular kind of research role that is adopted by the sociologist. There are several roles that are available, of course, and each has appealed to different sociologists. The most dominant has been that of the impartial observer, epitomizing a kind of neutrality and documentation ideal that is codified in the very ethics of the sociological profession. Lending itself to case study and to detailed observation of particular movement events, this role has appealed to those particularist sociologists who have been influenced in what we have called the social psychological or motivational intellectual tradition.

While sharing the case study methodology of the impartial observer, another role model has begun to be applied in recent years to the study of social movements. Here the sociologist, while using apparently neutral, even positivist methods in his analysis, becomes an apologist for the movement or movement event that she studies. The study of *Freedom Summer* by Doug McAdam (1988) provides a telling example of this new kind of role. On the one hand, McAdam describes in great detail the rigorous empirical methods that he has used both to identity the objects of his study and to corroborate his conclusions. And yet his sympathy for the movement, and even more perhaps for the individuals themselves who took part in the civil rights Freedom Summer of 1964, which will be discussed in detail in chapter 5, is apparent throughout. Indeed, the reader is left with the impression that the ideals of the white Freedom Summer activists continue to survive and even influence political life in the neoconservative 1980s. Quite a feat. McAdam plays here the role not merely of apologist, but of revivalist. By identifying with the movement he studies and by drawing out its continuing vitality even in the contemporary age, McAdam attempts to rekindle the sparks of a long gone movement. It is an exciting new role being played out here: the use of sociological analysis as catalyst for new political activity. Without perhaps even being aware of it himself, McAdam is playing a classical role of "movement intellectual," first developed in the European socialist movements of the nineteenth century, but now by McAdam in the United States of the 1980s confronted with a totally different set of contextual conditions.

A second important role among sociologists of social movements has been the organizational reformer. Here sociology has been part of a kind of social engineering that has been characteristic of postwar industrial societies on both sides of the Atlantic. Here empathy or identification has not been with a particular movement or movement event but rather with a social problem or sector. The rationalizing intellectuals of interwar Sweden – and the Keynesian inspired socialists in Britain in the 1940s and 1950s, as well as the best and the brightest who associated themselves with the new frontier of John F. Kennedy and the great society of Lyndon B. Johnson – all played the role of the sociological reformer, expert, and adviser. It is this role that conceptualizes social movements as organizational entitities, which focuses on their potential for reform and their mechanisms of recruitment. It is the sociologist as organizational expert who reduces the social movement to processes of resource mobilization.

Here as well, however, there are new identities and role models emerging. Piven and Cloward (1977), while sharing the intellectual traditions and even much of the conceptual framework of the resource mobilization sociologists, nonetheless illustrate a different role, namely that of the organizational activist. Their concern with social movements, or more specifically with poor people's movements, has grown out of an activist involvement in organizational development among welfare recipients. Their studies of other movements, and of their mechanisms of mobilization and development, are informed by an experience of organizational activity.

A third role, and one that has been especially noticeable in Europe among students of social movements, is the ideologist. Here the empathy with a class or a political party, which is a common subjective starting point for European sociologists, is transformed into a political activity within the academy. The sociologist studies the ideology of social movements at the same time as she attempts to contribute to that ideology. The role of ideologist is not dissimilar to that of grand theorist, for in both cases the sociologist removes herself from the actual movement being studied and instead evaluates its historical or deeper sociological significance or lack of significance (Eyerman 1984). But the ideologist is a partisan, identifying with an idealized movement, while the theorist is a professional academic, thus often seeing her role as a movement opponent, developing concepts that diminish the importance of movements in social change. While the organizational reformer, the activist observer, and the ideologist thus build their side-taking into their analyses, the documentalist, the expert, and the theorist are at pains to develop a detached neutrality that easily becomes animosity and opposition.

## From critique to comprehension

Our contextual reading of the students of social movements has, we hope, indicated some of the reasons behind the condition of fragmentation and specialization that characterizes the field. In this respect, of course, the sociology of social movements is no different from other areas of social analysis; and we would contend that similar readings of other sociological areas would also be an important step in their development. But now we must move on to the more constructive task of recombination, finding new concepts and theoretical starting points that allow us to understand social movements in a comprehensive way.

The reader has already been given some indication of how our analysis will proceed. Let us here, by way of concluding this chapter, sketch out in a more systematic manner the rest of what is to come. In chapter 2, we will expand and deepen our application of the sociology of knowledge to social movements by explicating the concept of cognitive praxis. By studying social movements as cognitive praxis we mean that they are producers of knowledge and that knowledge creation itself should be seen as a collective process. The dimensions of cognitive praxis have come to take on a number of different meanings as we have worked with them in our studies of environmentalism (Cramer et al., 1987; Eyerman and Jamison 1989). In chapter 3, we will apply this concept to other movements and to other "types of knowledge" than those which we studied previously.

It was Max Scheler who most ambitiously defined a program for the sociology of knowledge in the early 1920s (Scheler 1980). He said that the sociology of knowledge had been limited up to then by confining attention to certain more established forms of knowledge. If ways of knowing were to be compared across cultures, however, it was necessary to broaden the framework and to include not just organized or institutionalized knowledge, but also moral, religious, metaphysical, even mystical types of knowledge under the purview of the sociology of knowledge. This insight, and the program accompanying it, were largely lost to sociologists of knowledge as most of them have come to confine their interest to one type, usually one or another established scientific field. As the sociology of knowledge has been transformed into a sociology of science, on the one hand, and a sociology of social thought on the other, the broader ambitions that Scheler articulated have faded, only to be rediscovered by anthropologists seeking to explain differences in cultural worldviews and belief systems.

Our cognitive approach is rooted in this rediscovery, and attempts to grasp both formalized and informal modes of knowledge production within social movements. We want to argue that social movements are actually constituted by the cognitive praxis that is entailed in the articulation of their historical projects. The actual types of knowledge that a social movement articulates or is interested in obviously varies from movement to movement. Thus, while environmental movements tend toward the more formalized natural and technical sciences, and have contributed to both theoretical and empirical fields in ecology and technology, the cognitive praxis of the American civil rights movement was almost entirely informal, what Scheler would have called religious, moral, and spiritual. Civil rights activists articulated moral principles and

spirituality. Their cognitive praxis was thus rooted in a vastly different intellectual space and tradition than that of environmentalism.
Comparing the two will hopefully bring out the range of applicabil-
ity of our concept as well as the value of the concept in linking
concerns from each of the now dominant but fragmented discourses
analyzed above.

Cognitive praxis is the most basic of our concepts. It provides
what we have called in our earlier work the core identity of a social
movement. It is a kind of deep structure that allows us to draw
certain boundaries around a movement as it develops over time, as
well as to evaluate the current status and potential of actual movements. Our second major concept, movement intellectual, has a
different status in being oriented more to actors than to movements
as a whole. The two concepts are connected in that it is movement
intellectuals, as historical actors, who make visible the underlying
cognitive praxis.

The term itself is derived from the insights of Antonio Gramsci
and others about the formation of intellectuals (Gramsci 1971). It
was by reflecting on their own role that Gramsci and before him
Lukács thematized and theorized a form of social practice (Lukács
1972). The sociological study of intellectuals has largely tended to
focus on roles and role models, and the relation between those
roles and larger social forces has tended to be avoided. But if we
are to understand where intellectuals, and especially new intellectual roles and types, come from, that is, what social forces have led
to their formation, then we must return to the reflective mode of
thinking. In particular, we must examine in some detail how social
movements create spaces for new types of intellectuals to emerge.
This we will do in chapter 4, by reviewing the relations of intellectuals to contemporary social movements, and also by examining the
earlier relations that were formed in the nineteenth and early
twentieth centuries.

As such, our concepts answer the challenge posed by social
movements to sociology. They encompass, we will indicate, the
perspectives of others while not being reducible to any of them. We
will not reject the findings of other sociologists in developing our
concepts but we hope to show how each of them has been limited in
her understanding by the limited character of her concepts.

# 2

# Social movements as cognitive praxis

## Introduction

There is something fundamental missing from the sociology of social movements, something that falls between the categories of the various schools and is left out of their various conceptualizations. That something is what we mean by cognitive praxis. It is not that sociologists of social movements are not aware of a certain cognitive dimension in the activities of the movements they study, but it is something that they are unable to theorize in that it remains marginal to their main concerns. As it is for most social movement activists themselves, the cognitive interests and activities of the movements being studied by sociologists are largely taken for granted. They are the unreflected assumptions of analysis rather than the objects of investigation.

The problem begins in the very act of defining a social movement. For the particularists and for most resource mobilization sociologists, a social movement is defined empirically. Indeed it is seldom defined at all, but rather it is studied as an empirical phenomenon. For the particularists, a movement is seen from the vantage point of the actor and thus definition is made by those being studied: self-definition. For the resource mobilization school of thought, a movement is defined in operational terms: organizations are distinguished from sectors, or industries, and the movement dissolves into the particular mechanisms of mobilization and recruitment that are being analyzed. In a recent survey article, Charles Tilly has written that "the proper analogy to a social movement is neither a party nor a union but a political campaign. What we call a social movement actually consists in a series of demands or challenges to power-holders in the name of a social category that lacks an established political position" (Tilly 1985: 735–6). Instead of focusing on cognitive activity, the meaning of a movement for Tilly is to be read out of its particular "framework of action repertoires." A movement is what it does and how it does it, not what its members think and why they think the ideas that they do.

In this empirical universe populated by most American sociologists, knowledge, and for many, even identity are seen as nonempirical objects and thus largely outside of the sociologist's area of competence. What we refer to as cognitive praxis is seen through the prism of "packages of ideas" or clusters of issues, or, perhaps most ambitiously, as organizational ideologies or profiles (Klandermans et al., 1988). But the problem, as we see it, is that knowledge becomes disembodied; it is relegated to a largely marginal, ephemeral or superstructural level of reality, and not to the centrality of movement identity formation where we contend it belongs. The identity of the movement becomes disinterested, stripped of its driving ideas, its cognitive meaning. The particular historical interests that a movement aims to further are not analyzed in the process of being formed, as a central component of movement praxis. The knowledge interests of a social movement are frozen into static, ready-formed packages, providing the issues or ideologies around which movements mobilize resources or socialize individuals. Cognitive praxis is invisible for eyes that are directed elsewhere or focused through the wrong paradigmatic eyeglasses. For the currently dominant paradigms of social movement analysis, it is other components of movement praxis – the tactical, strategic, organizational, even emotional actions and interactions – which are subjected to the analytical gaze of the sociologist. They are thus not seen as important sources for new cognitive developments in the sciences and/or everyday life.

For many of the European students of social movements, the difficulties are of a different sort. Here it is the political meaning of a movement that is of most importance, its sociohistorical rather than its cognitive identity. What Jean Cohen calls identity theorists are those sociologists who define social movements as attempts to create new collective identities. The identities are, however, not derived from studying the cognitive praxis of movements themselves, but rather drawn from theories of social change and philosophies of history. Lurking behind the identity theorists are the classical social theorists of the nineteenth century, and behind them the positivist and idealist philosophies of Comte and Hegel. As such, identity in the sense used by many European sociologists is something superimposed on a social movement and used as a standard of evaluation to judge their potential and historical significance, even their status as a social movement. Thus Alain Touraine, after investigating the French antinuclear energy movement, concluded that the movement was not a real social movement: it was not involved in the struggle for what he terms "historicity" (Touraine 1983).

In a similar vein, many political writers and social thinkers on both sides of the Atlantic have sought to characterize the ideological messages of the socalled new social movements. Carl Boggs (1985) has, for instance, attempted to place some of the new movements within what he calls a post-Marxist discourse. The terms of the discourse are, to a certrain extent, derived from the activity of the movements, but they are interpreted as the ideological results of the movement, and are thus seen as products rather than processes. In any case, they are not studied in formation, as cognitive praxis. We do not challenge the legitimacy or even the value of such an exercise; our point is merely that Boggs and others are not so much analyzing the movements as incorporating them into their own ideals and ideologies. Such readings of social movements are by now rather common. The primarily ideological writings of, for instance, André Gorz (1982) in France and Rudolf Bahro (1984) in Germany can be considered significant political statements, pointing toward a postindustrial or even postmaterial future (Frankel 1987). But they unfortunately contribute little to our understanding of the actual cognitive significance of social movements. What gets lost from view is the dynamic role, the mediating role that movements play in what might be termed the social shaping of knowledge. Thus, while the empirical sociologists largely neglect the cognitive praxis of social movements because it cannot be easily reduced to empirical data, for the more theoretically minded the knowledge interests of the new social movements are transformed into ideological positions or organizational programs.

Jean Cohen has suggested, as part of her attempt to synthesize the different schools of social movement theory, that the "theory of communicative action" developed by Jürgen Habermas "allows one to see how the paradigms of collective action [i.e., resource mobilization and identity theory] ... can be complementary." She distinguishes conceptually between normative and communicative interaction and contends that, at least on the abstract level, a concept of communicative interaction can inform all theories of social movements. "It refers to the linguistically mediated, intersubjective process through which actors *establish* their interpersonal relations and coordinate their action, through negotiating definitions of the situation (norms) and coming to an agreement" (Cohen 1985: 707). Such a concept, Cohen writes, obviously forgetting Blumer's symbolic interactionism, has not been applied directly to the analysis of social movements. In any case, the process of communicative interaction has not been explored empirically – indeed, this is one of the points in her criticism of Habermas's views on social movements. Our approach to reading social movements aims to examine historical and contemporary movements from the vantage point of such communicative interaction. It is what we mean by cognitive praxis.

Perhaps closest to our position among contemporary students of social movements is the Italian sociologist Alberto Melucci, who sees the challenge of the new social movements in primarily "symbolic" terms. Drawing on the terminology of semiotics and his own practice as a psychotherapist, Melucci sees the identity formation of social movements as a kind of social dramaturgy; the "movements no longer operate as characters but as *signs*," Melucci writes. "They do this in the sense that they translate their action into symbolic challenges that upset the dominant cultural codes and reveal their irrationality and partiality by acting at the levels (of information and communication) at which the new forms of technocratic power also operate" (Melucci 1988: 249). Social movements make power visible, Melucci argues, and they challenge the dominant meaning systems or symbols of contemporary everyday life.

Our conceptualization of social movements as cognitive praxis also seeks to grasp the symbolic, or expressive, significance of social movements. But we see that significance not merely as a challenge to established power, but also and more so as a socially constructive force, as a fundamental determinant of human knowledge. The cognitive praxis of social movements is not just social drama; it is, we might say, the social action from where new knowledge originates. It is from, among other places, the cognitive praxis of social movements that science and ideology – as well as everyday knowledge – develop new perspectives. In order to see that formative influence, however, it is necessary to read social movements in a particular cognitive way.

## A sociological conception of knowledge

Knowledge for us is a fundamental category, providing the basis or the working materials for what Berger and Luckmann (1967) termed the social construction of reality. Society is constructed by "re-cognition," by recurrent acts of knowing that go on all the time. Knowledge in this perspective is not only or even primarily the systematized, formalized knowledge of the academic world, nor (merely) the scientific knowledge produced by sanctioned professionals. It is rather the broader cognitive praxis that informs all social activity. It is thus both formal and informal, objective and subjective, moral and immoral, and, most importantly, professional and popular.

This broad conception of knowledge was characteristic of the period between the First World War and the Second World War when the social movements of fascism and communism were seen by many intellectuals to challenge the notions of enlightened reason that were central to Western civilization. Critical theory and sociology of knowledge were both born in a public space carved out by the social movements of the 1920s and 1930s. The Marxist intellectuals of the Frankfurt School sought to combat what Max Horkheimer was to call the "eclipse of reason" with a new conceptualization of consciousness in which intellectual activity was seen as dialectically related to social praxis (Horkheimer 1974).

The general ambition of the sociology of knowledge, as developed by Max Scheler and Karl Mannheim, was more academic; it was to find a synthesis between "objectivist" and "subjectivist" conceptions of knowledge in a kind of sociological intersubjectivity. The sociology of knowledge was an explicit attempt to rise above the passsions of extremist belief and develop a rational understanding of all types of knowledge, both scientific and ideological. Indeed, as it came to be developed by Karl Mannheim (1948), a detached sociology of knowledge and a group of dispassionate free-floating intellectuals were seen as crucially necessary in an age in which knowledge had become all too emotional, all too partisan.

The sociology of knowledge that Mannheim developed was, in

many ways, constrained by its context. From our perspective, it went too far in narrowing the original Schelerian ambition to a sociological subfield (Jamison 1982). Our conceptualization attempts to recombine the "precision" of Mannheim with the critical social theory of Lukács, Horkheimer, Marcuse, and Adorno, whose more critical conception of knowledge developed in the 1930s in a kind of opposition to the sociology of knowledge. As such, we want to reconnect sociology of knowledge to social theory. Based on Marxism as well as on German idealistic philosophy, Lukács and the later Frankfurt School sought to analyze the relations between social change and social consciousness. Rather than starting from the ideas themselves as did the sociologists of knowledge, the critical Marxists started from society and attempted to elucidate, as well as produce, the kind of knowledge that was necessary for revolutionary change. They attempted to articulate an alternative to the bourgeois rationality of capitalist society; by developing reflection and dialectical thinking as sociological tools, Horkheimer, Marcuse, Adorno, Fromm, and the other critical theorists sought to create an alternative to the sociology of knowledge, as well as to positivist thought more generally (Jay 1973). They also sought to reconnect to the critical, more anthropological conceptions of knowledge of the early Marx in opposition to the scientific Marxism that had so much come to dominate the communist movement.[1]

For both the sociologists of knowledge and the critical theorists, knowledge was seen as the collective creation of social groups; it emerged on the basis of what might be termed sociohistorical interest. Common to both interwar projects was an ambition to contextualize the development of consciousness, to identify the social agents of new forms of knowledge. The challenge to universal reason embodied in the social movements inspired many intellectuals to reflect on the social basis of reason and to seek means to defend and eventually revitalize the social conditions necessary for the further development of rational thought.

## Rediscovering sociological conceptions of knowledge: the 1960s and beyond

In the postwar era, knowledge has tended to be reduced by sociology to one or another of its component parts; there are thus sociologists of scientific knowledge, sociologists of religious belief systems, sociologists of everyday knowledge, and even sociologists of sociological knowledge. And, as with the study of social movements, sociologists of knowledge have tended to approach their subject at different levels of abstraction, with grand theorists at one extreme and students of particular knowers or knowledge contexts at the other.

The rediscovery of the sociology of knowledge in the 1960s was both externally and internally generated. On the one hand, it grew out of the student movement and the new left, perhaps especially among natural science and engineering students. The radical concerns of some scientists, participation in the antiwar movement, and the ensuing challenges to academic authority led to a rediscovery of the debates of the 1920s and 1930s, and to a new literature of "radical science" and "radical philosophy" published in new journals and eventually in books (for instance, Rose and Rose 1975). Influential also were the works of Herbert Marcuse, in particular his *One-Dimensional Man* (1964) which presented a modern version of the critique of technological rationality for a new generation. As one of the participants in the early development of critical theory in the 1930s, Marcuse represented, as well, a personal connection between the generations. The positivism debate in Germany between Karl Popper and Theodor Adorno also played a role in bringing the legacy of critical theory into the consciousness of social scientists. By the end of the 1960s, the criticism of science within the student movement and new left had inspired a new movement of environmental activism and also led many scientists out of the laboratories to create courses in "social responsibility" and eventually programs and departments in science studies.

Internally, the rediscovery of sociological conceptions of knowledge was inspired by a number of influential works which challenged the limited and highly fragmented views of knowledge that dominated postwar philosophy, history, and sociology of science. Books such as Thomas Kuhn's *Structure of Scientific Revolutions* (1962) and Berger and Luckmann's *Social Construction of Reality* (1967) pointed to an area of sociological investigation that had been neglected but which seemed to call out for detailed investigation. In the 1970s, growing numbers of sociologists challenged the then dominant institutional approach of Robert Merton (1957) and Joseph Ben-David (1971) and called for sociological analysis of the contents of science, as well as its institutions.

If we are to consider social movements in terms of their cognitive praxis, it becomes necessary to recombine what are now disparate discourses in the sociology of knowledge. Even with the new perspectives that have emerged since the 1960s, the sociology of knowledge remains divided between those who study professional, scientific knowledge and those who study "everyday" knowledge. The division has led to separate theories, separate audiences, and separate social functions. It has also meant that social movements have difficulty finding a place in the conceptual and explanatory frameworks developed by sociologists of knowledge. Cognition is seen either as the work of professional cognizers or the work of everyone; and although the connections between the various types of knowledge production are recognized, they are seldom the topic of any sustained treatment. That is what we aim to do in the rest of this book. What we suggest is a mediating role for social movements both in the transformation of everyday knowledge into professional knowledge, and, perhaps even more importantly, in providing new contexts for the reinterpretation of professional knowledge. As such, we seek to link the new, micro-level approaches of sociologists of science to the broader macro-level approaches of (critical) social theorists.

The sociologists of science have sought to show how scientific knowledge is socially constructed (Knorr-Cetina and Mulkay 1983). They have gone into the laboratories, either as anthropologists visiting a foreign planet, or as ethnomethodologists analyzing ritualized behavior, or as discourse analysts decoding scientific texts. Sociologists have uncovered the processes of negotiation by which truth is established in scientific research, disclosing how scientific concepts and theories are manufactured according to complicated actor networks and institutional frameworks (Latour 1987).

In almost all cases, however, the sociologists of science have left the broader society outside their purview. The laboratory, or the scientific workplace, has become a surrogate society, a micro-level society that either represents a particular empirical universe of its own or is made to stand as a kind of microcosm for broader macro-level processes of social interaction. In both cases, however, the contextualizations of the sociologists of scientific knowledge have become ever more internal, the contexts of relevance being limited to the institutional and organizational frameworks within which scientists work.

On the epistemological level, social constructivism has led to a relativization of scientific truth. The attempt to demystify science or, as the title of one recent volume puts it, to take "science off the pedestal," has led to a challenge to traditional, more positivist conceptions of knowledge (Chu and Chubin 1989). Where science was traditionally conceived as rational pursuit of valid knowledge, or reliable knowledge, or, perhaps most precisely, verifiable knowledge, the new sociology of science has shown that knowledge production is a social phenomenon. Among other things, this has raised the possibility of a social epistemology by which the "truth" of scientific knowledge is seen as dependent on its social context (Fuller 1988).

It has proved difficult, however, to move from the internal contexts of research laboratories and scientific institutions to the broader society; that is, the social construction of knowledge has not yet taken broader social forces into account in developing its social epistemologies. Where do new scientific ideas come from? From which social actors, through which social processes, at which historical moments do new approaches to scientific knowledge emerge? On these fundamental questions, the new sociology of science has as yet little to say. By focusing almost exclusively on scientific research at a micro level, the field has – perhaps unwittingly – made it all but impossible to answer the more fundamental question: where does scientific knowledge come from in the first place? In not problematizing this question, the sociologists of science appear to accept some of the assumptions that they criticize, that scientific knowledge is the product of individual genius and inspiration and that its validity is derived from internal, intra-scientific criteria rather than from the wider social context.

What is needed, from our perspective, is a closing of the gap between the new sociology of science and the sociology of social movements. Certain preliminary steps have been taken, such as the recent work on the sociology of technology by Wiebe Bijker and others (Bijker et al., 1987). Here, the creation of technological artifacts is seen as the work of social networks of actors, and the values and interests of those actors are seen as having a fundamental determining role in the development of technological knowledge. Similarly, anthropologists and sociologists inspired by Foucault have looked at the relations between knowledge production and political power, exploring mechanisms of institutionalization as instruments of social control and discipline (Law 1986). The focus on intellectual strategies, so central to the work of Pierre Bourdieu, has also begun to influence sociologists, and has directed

attention to the subtle forms of interaction between social stratifica-
tion and knowledge production (Bourdieu 1988). In many respects,
this approach echoes the Marxian attempts to attribute knowledge
production to class interests.

Our cognitive approach to social movements is an attempt to
integrate these diverse threads into a contextual theory of knowledge. Drawing on a synthetic or interactionist tradition of social
theorizing, represented in recent years especially by the work of
Habermas (1987b) and Giddens (1985), our perspective seeks to
reconnect an individual or psychological level of analysis to a collective or sociological level of analysis. We aim, in other words, at
providing a social theory which focuses on the interactions between
individual, collective, and macro societal practices. In the case of
social movements, this interaction, we suggest, can best be understood as cognitive praxis. Indeed, it is our claim that a social
movement *is* its cognitive praxis, that is, what distinguishes one
movement from another, but also, and more importantly, what
gives a social movement its significance for broader social processes.

Our focus on cognitive praxis is directed both to sociologists of
knowledge and to sociologists of social movements. On the one
hand, we want to provide an important "missing link" in the social
construction of science. Scientific knowledge, we contend, is directly dependent on social movements in a variety of ways. In the
seventeenth century, the very idea of science, as experimental
philosophy, emerged in the context of the religious movements of
revolutionary Britain (Webster 1975). And in the eighteenth and
nineteenth centuries, science after science, discipline after discipline emerged as a result of, or in answer to, questions about
nature and society that were raised by social movements. In our
own time, as we will argue in detail in the chapters that follow, new
fields, new conceptual frameworks, new intellectual roles, new
scientific problems, new scientific ideas themselves are directly
attributable to the "knowledge interests" of social movements.
Through what we call movement intellectuals, who are formed as
intellectuals in social spaces constituted by social movements, new
ideas are able to be articulated.

On the other hand, our cognitive reading of social movements
can help resolve the fragmentation that currently plagues the
sociology of social movements discussed in the previous chapter. A
social epistemology that directs attention to the role of social move-

ments as cognitive actors can avoid the polarization between grand theories and particularist studies. It can also correct the instrumental bias that is so characteristic of resource mobilization and its many variants. We want to read social movements as producers of knowledge, not as rational operators in a world of competing movement industries.

## Social movements as knowledge producers

The collective articulation of movement identity can be likened to a process of social learning in which movement organizations act as structuring forces, opening a space in which creative interaction between individuals can take place. At a certain point in time, the interaction takes on a further dimension, as different organizations together carve out an actual societal space, transforming what began as interpersonal interests into interorganizational concerns, that is, from individual into wider social terms. This transition from a formative to an organizational phase, we contend, is what distinguishes social movements from action groups or single-issue protest organizations. A social movement is not one organization or one particular special interest group. It is more like a cognitive territory, a new conceptual space that is filled by a dynamic interaction between different groups and organizations. It is through tensions betweeen different organizations over defining and acting in that conceptual space that the (temporary) identity of a social movement is formed.

This does not mean that social movements are only learning processes; but it rather means that the particular character of a movement, what distinguishes it from other movements and what sets it off in time, is its cognitive praxis. Having said this, it is apparent that cognitive praxis does not come readymade to a social movement. It is precisely in the creation, articulation, formulation of new thoughts and ideas – new knowledge – that a social movement defines itself in society. This means that other elements of social movement activity are not so much ignored as reinterpreted. As we will indicate in our case study on the American civil rights movement, campaigns or demonstrations are of interest to our cognitive approach not as particular historical events or moments but as illustrations of the formative tensions of cognitive praxis.

Cognitive praxis is, we contend, the core activity of a social movement. In analyzing it, it is useful to think in terms of the phases, or stages, of development that are so well established in the study of social movements. It is generally recognized (for instance, Smelser 1962, McAdam 1982) that social movements go through a kind of lifecycle, from gestation to formation and consolidation. Social movements seldom emerge spontaneously; instead they require long periods of preparation both at the individual, group, and societal level. No social movement emerges until there is a political opportunity available, a context of social problem as well as a context of communication, opening up the potential for problem articulation and knowledge dissemination. Not every social problem, however, generates a social movement; only those that strike a fundamental chord, that touch basic tensions in a society have the potential for generating a social movement. As such, our approach tends to limit the number of social movements to those especially "significant" movements which redefine history, which carry the historical "projects" that have normally been attributed to social classes. A movement conceptualizes fundamental contradictions or tensions in society – what Smelser called structural strains: in our day, for instance, the tensions between man and nature, between the sexes, as well as between "masters" and "slaves." Yet not even that is enough to determine the emergence of a social movement. Not until the theme has been articulated, not until the tensions have been formulated in a new conceptual space can a social movement come into being, and this is a very uncertain process involving many contingencies. Our point here is that among those contingencies the ability of "movement intellectuals" to formulate the knowledge interests of the emergent social movement is particularly crucial. Exactly what this means will be the subject of chapter 4.

At the same time, no social movement can emerge until individuals are ready to take part in it, willing to transform what C. Wright Mills (1963) called private troubles into public problems, as well as to enter into a process of collective identity formation. No matter how objectively necessary a social movement might appear to be, real individuals must make it happen. All of these levels of motivation are significant in the later stages of social movement lifecycles, as well. The longevity of a social movement is largely the result of how long a society takes it seriously as a political force, and this, in turn, depends on the commitment of individual actors, their creative use of strategy and tactics, the response of the established political institutions, and the willingness and capacity of the entire social formation to absorb, incorporate, of reject the "message" of the movement.

Cognitive praxis does not appear all at once, but emerges over time; and in conceptualizing its cyclical development, it can be valuable to draw on theories of other cyclical processes, such as those studied by students of technological innovation (Dosi et al., 1988). Students of technology have come to see innovation as a process, often starting with the discovery of new ideas in the scientific research laboratory. From the "pool" of ideas only some, usually for economic reasons, are selected for a further stage of "applied research" and development, which takes place within a corporate space of commercially oriented establishments. Those ideas that actually lead to useful products are then transferred from the realm of research and development to a third stage of marketing, or diffusion of innovations.

Thinking of the cognitive praxis of social movements as a kind of product cycle, moving from discovery/articulation through application/specification to diffusion/institutionalization is not meant to imply any mechanical logic to social movement praxis. Rather, it is meant to suggest a congruence between different kinds of social learning processes. Social movement activists "learn by doing" as much as professional engineers; and their cognitive praxis should be expected to reflect accumulated experience of the past as much as, if not more so, than the cognitive praxis of established knowledge producers. In the case of social movements, this experience is not only that of individual actors or even of the collective group composing the particular movement, but is as well the experience of previous movements and – not least – other movements acting concurrently.

Looking at social movements as cognitive praxis means seeing knowledge creation as a collective process. It means that knowledge is not the "discovery" of an individual genius, nor is it the determined outcome of systemic interactions within an established Research and Development system. Knowledge is instead the product of a series of social encounters, within movements, between movements, and even more importantly perhaps, between movements and their established opponents.

These creative learning processes of cognitive praxis occur on several levels. They take place in the unpredictable and often unintended interaction between movement activists in planning future and reflecting on past actions. Here the question is often how the project is to be operationalized, how a particular campaign or demonstration can best be used to put the message across. The heated debates over meeting agendas and demonstration slogans and specific organizational activities that are the stuff of all social movements are, for us, examples of cognitive praxis.

Other examples take place in the interaction between movement groups and their opponents, in the myriad of arenas of confrontation and dialogue that make up the public sphere. Here the cognitive praxis is often more strategic than communicative, more instrumental than expressive. In confronting the state or other agents of established power, social movements innovate tactics and organization forms. Indeed, a social movement can be thought of as one large social innovation, a new actor in society representing previously latent interests. In this, as in many other respects, there is nothing automatically progressive about social movements; as history itself is open and often regresses, social movements can re-act, as well as act, mobilizing interests that represent regressive as well as progressive values. Their ideological orientation need not affect their creativity; all social movements are producers of knowledge.

Cognitive praxis also takes place in interactions between contemporary social movements and "old" ones, in the direct sense of the interplay and competition between old and new social movements in the same time and place, as well as between contemporary social movements and the wide range of social movements of the past. Social movements are active in the continual reinvention of tradition, and in the recombination of the values or interests of past movements. As we will see in the chapters that follow, this recombination involves both the reformulation of concepts and projects as well as the reinterpretation of intellectual roles and practices.

What focusing on the cognitive praxis of social movements means is to see them as creative forces in society, as sources of inspiration as well as new knowledge. This focus has not been entirely left out of social movement research. As we discussed in the previous chapter, structural-functional theorists of collective behavior with an interest in social change like Smelser have looked at the role social movements play in signaling areas of social "strain" for political elites. Identity theorists focus on the codes or symbols that are expressed by social movements in their various actions and activities. But nowhere is this interest in cognitive praxis systematized or connected to a contextual theory of knowledge.

In order to read social movements as cognitive praxis, we must look behind some of the fashionable reductionist perspectives among sociologists of knowledge and reconsider the totality of knowledge "types." It is certainly a positive achievement that Kuhn and others have opened up scientific knowledge to sociological analysis; it is valuable indeed to understand the social processes in scientific discovery and the social interests that condition scientific development. But a perhaps unintended effect has been a relative neglect of nonscientific knowledge. This is understandable enough in our highly scientific age, but it does represent a clear narrowing of sociological focus. And it mades it difficult to see the role that social movements play in the development of knowledge.

As we shall see, the cognitive praxis of many social movements lies between the disparate types of knowledge; social movements create new types of knowledge as well as recombine or connect previously separate types of knowledge with each other. Indeed, we want to argue that much if not all new knowledge emanates from the cognitive praxis of social movements, that new ideas both in and out of science are the often unconscious results of new knowledge interests of social movements. But this formative influence can only be uncovered if we have a broad notion of knowledge to begin with.

### "Reading" social movements cognitively: a note on method

Let us conclude this chapter by trying to draw some methodological conclusions. How can a conception of social movements as cognitive praxis be put to analytical use? What does it mean to "read" social movements in a cognitive way?

As mentioned earlier, a cognitive approach to social movements means having a processual focus, seeing social movements as processes in formation. One of the main barriers to recognizing social movements as producers of knowledge is the widespread tendency to reify them, to identify social movements with organizations, parties, sects, institutions, etc. Social movements are all too often reduced to specific empirical phenomena, and as such their "theory" as well as their inner dynamic fades from consideration. We contend, however, that the distinctiveness of social movements, indeed their very historical significance, lies in their impermanence, disorganization, transience, in short in their motion. A movement moves, it can be seen (for instance, Touraine 1981) as a kind of transition from one historical conjuncture to another; and, as such, its cognitive praxis can only be identified in formation. Once the ideas engendering movement become formalized either within the scientific community or in the established political culture, they have for all intents and purposes left the space of the movement behind.

This impermanent quality of social movements is central to our approach. A movement, by definition, lives and dies, or, more colorfully perhaps, it withers away as its cognitive project disintegrates into its various component parts and they become either adopted or discarded. Movements create for a time a space for social activity, a public space for interest articulation. Usually originating in protest of the established order, a social movement creates a public space that did not previously exist. And although movements usually involve the creation of organizations or the renovation of institutions, it is important not to mistake the one for the other. Organizations can be thought of as vehicles or instruments for carrying or transporting or even producing the movement's meaning. But the meaning, we hasten to add, should not be reduced to the medium. The meaning, or core identity, is rather the cognitive space that the movement creates, a space for new kinds of ideas and relationships to develop.

In the following chapter, we will illustrate these general claims with examples drawn from particular movements. We will refer both to our own research on contemporary environmental movements, as well as to historical experiences in the socalled old social movements of the working class. Before "reading" the empirical material, however, it might be useful to say something more about our particular methods of reading.

First of all, we read selectively, or, more precisely, we read epistemologically. Our approach does not claim to be comprehensive: we do not mean to be able to explain why social movements happen or, for that matter, why particular individuals choose to take part in them. What interests us is what a social movement represents for the development of human knowledge. And this knowledge, as discussed above, is both formal and informal, referring to organized scientific knowledge as well as broader aspects of political and social consciousness. Through our examples, we want to provide insights into the following questions: Which new ideas are produced in social movements and how do we go about characterizing those ideas? What do particular social movements contribute to social processes of knowledge production? And finally, and perhaps most centrally, what common processes or mechanisms of cognitive praxis can we identify in social movements from different historical periods and different countries? Our attempt to answer the final question is also our contribution to the broader discussion among sociologists about the character of social movements.

Secondly, we read critically. On the one hand, we distance ourselves from the movements we study, but the sociological distance that we seek to establish is not the objectivity that so many empirical sociologists strive to achieve. It is more like a qualified subjectivity, an evaluative or reflective distance that comes from our identification with a critical theory of society, or more broadly with an interpretative or qualitative tradition of sociology. Critical distance means placing movements in context, but it also means subjecting their praxis to reflection, to theorization. We try to locate the basic beliefs of a social movement, attempting, through critical reflection, to get to the core set of assumptions that gives a particular movement its identity. This means that our critical method of reading is a sort of deconstruction; we decompose the "text" of a movement into its component parts, its various dimensions, uncovering a hidden reality behind appearance. But unlike deconstructionists we also try to put the components back together again. More precisely, our critical method offers historical, contextual understanding for activist and scholar alike. We make no epistemological claims for the truth value of the reality that we understand, nor do we claim any privileged insight for our interpretation. Ours is a social epistemology, by which the truth of knowledge is contingent on the social context in which it is practiced. In relation to movements and movement activists, we aim to be interpreters rather than legislators (Bauman 1987). In relation to sociologists of social movements, we aim to be expansionist readers rather than reductionist analyzers. We attempt to reconstruct or re-member the core identity of a social movement in the broad, historically informed context of a theory of social movements.

Cognitive praxis is an operational term, but it is also we contend, an empirical term. It is however, a particular type of empirical phenomenon. Cognitive praxis takes place and can be studied empirically, but one should not necessarily look for it in the heads of the activists involved in social movements. As we discovered in our study of environmental movements, what we then called the "knowledge interests" of the movements under investigation did not present themselves to us readyformed. They had to be sifted out of movement documents and activist recollections, and their emergence and development had to be reconstructed. But they were not exclusively our creations, superimposed on the movement from preconceived ideologies or beliefs. Nor were they planted by us in the heads of those we interviewed, and then later harvested in a fit of self discovery. The cognitive praxis, or knowledge interests, of the new environmental movements were rather seen in the context of a social theory, a space of our own sociological creation, between actors and organizations. In short, cognitive praxis is there, but its dimensions must be found by someone looking for them. They guide actors but not necessarily consciously or explicitly. Even more importantly, they cannot exist without the actors being guided by them. They are a kind of glue that makes a social movement what it is. What exactly this implies is what we hope to illustrate in the next chapter.

We can conceive of social movements as cognitive praxis also because we read social movements historically; we read social movements in retrospect. We distance ourselves not merely through a technique of analysis, but also through time. In order to understand the historical projects of social movements, it is necessary to see them from within a dialectical theory of history; this means that social movements are at once conditioned by the historical contexts in which they emerge, their particular time and place, and, in turn, affect that context through their cognitive and political praxis. As the opponents of established patterns of thought and of politics, social movements are creators of history: out of their oppositional stance, their utopian critique, new historical opportunities arise and new syntheses or recombinations take place. But each movement or period of movement has its own historical meaning. There are continuities between old and new social movements, but there are also substantial differences.

History is not imposed on movements, but it conditions them, it provides their starting points as well as their range of operation. This means that the dimensions of cognitive praxis must be reconstructed in the context of their actualization. Our retrospective reading focuses on the interplay between movement identity formation and long-term social processes, that is, between internal knowledge push and external political pull. We read the tension between communicative and instrumental action, to speak with Habermas, or the interplay between cognitive development and structuration of society, to speak with Giddens.

It needs to be remembered that all social movements, according to our way of thinking, are transitory phenomena. The space they create is temporary, and continually invaded by other social actors. And yet, for a time, the cognitive praxis of a social movement or perhaps more accurately, of a period of social movement, open up new opportunities for thought. For us, it is less important to label particular social movements and distinguish them from each other, or to legislate when a period of social movement begins and ends, than it is to find common denominators within movements and among different movements in a particular time period. Our point is not that definition is unimportant but that it is less important than identifying the dimensions of cognitive praxis. Arbitrary or empirically based typologies and definitions often make it difficult to find what "different" movements have in common. We share with many American sociologists the assumption that social movements are empirical phemomena that exist independently of our theories about them; but we also share the ambition of many European sociologists to uncover a deeper meaning in social movement. That deeper meaning is what we mean by mean by cognitive praxis.

There are thus historical periods characterized by social movement and there are periods of institutionalization and absorption, when movements more or less disappear as their ideas are incorporated to re-form established patterns, or are discarded; the knowledge and the activists that were a social movement are then assimilated or rejected in processes of social reconstitution. Empirically, social movements exist only through their particular historical manifestations. They emerge, take organizational form, and are more or less successful in their attempts to affect political and social processes.

The concept of cognitive praxis allows us to specify and distinguish among particular movements which occur contemporaneously within periods of social movement. Thus, one can distinguish, for example, the environmental movement from the student movements which more or less directly preceded it, showing the continuities and differences in their respective cognitive praxis as well as between activists and political strategies. In periods of social movement, particular movements tend to feed off and create each other, as well as producing, conceptually and practically, their opposition. We will return to this in chapter 4 when discussing the articulating role of movement intellectuals.

Gauging the relative success or failure of social movements, that is, measuring their ability to affect and transform established patterns of behavior has been an important issue in the empirical study of social movements. From our perspective, movement success is paradoxical. On the empirical level, the success or failure of a particular movement usually depends on its ability to mobilize resources and to exploit the "opportunity structures" of the surrounding political culture to achieve its strategic aims. In a broader historical sense, however, the success of a social movement depends on the effective diffusion of its knowledge production; but diffusion depends upon there being sufficient time and space for a movement identity to be articulated. Some movements are successful in one way while being failures in the other.[2]

Thus, our reading of social movements focuses not so much on causation or political effect as on message: what is the kind of historical project that a social movement articulates? As our historical examples will indicate, we are not uninterested in understanding why social movements appear, but establishing cause or providing causal explanation is of less importance than deepening understanding. In this regard, our approach is more hermeneutic than positivistic: our aim is to understand rather than explain, although the two ambitions are often difficult to separate. In any case, our interest in explanation is of a more conditional character; social movements, we contend, are conditioned rather than caused by historical and contextual "factors." Movements create themselves and their own particular movement spaces, but their praxis is conditioned by the society around them.

Our historical examples will point to some of the ways in which this conditioning takes place. The social movements of the nineteenth century emerged at particular conjunctures; although they exist as local groups or even organizations throughout the century, it is in particular periods – in most countries, the 1830s and 1840s and then again in the 1880s and 1890s – that there is social movement. This is, of course, a matter of opinion; and there is by no means consensus among historians about the range or the appropriate connotations of the term social movement. Some apply it to any sign of popular mobilization, while others specify exacting criteria. From our perspective, the criteria of social movement are cognitive: that is, a social movement must articulate identifiable cognitive products or types of knowledge. But we also define social movements dynamically: they are, by our definition, impermanent, transient phenomena, which means that there are ebbs and flows, cycles if you will, of movement activity. Indeed, we could even talk of latent and active periods, or weak and strong periods, but the point would be the same; movements do not last forever, they come for a time, carve out their movement space, and get eventually "pulled" back into the society, as the space they create gets occupied by other social forces.

# 3

# Dimensions of cognitive praxis

## Environmental movements as cognitive praxis

In our studies of environmentalism, we identified three dimensions of cognitive praxis in the new environmental movements in Sweden, Denmark, and the Netherlands (Jamison et al., 1990). In all three countries, we found a similar set of ideas and conceptions among environmentalists which we divided into three types, or dimensions of "knowledge interest": cosmological, technological, and organizational. The cosmological dimension referred to the basic assumptions or beliefs derived from systems ecology, which all environmental activists took more or less for granted. The technological dimension referred to the specific topics of environmental protest, as well as the alternative techniques that have been developed in, for example, renewable energy and biodynamic agriculture. The organizational dimension referred to the anti-elitism that environmentalism shares with most of the other new social movements, an ambition to deprofessionalize expertise and develop new, more democratic forms of knowledge production. The ideas themselves – an ecological worldview, a small-scale alternative technology, and a democratic "science for the people" – had been formulated in the 1960s by more or less established scientists and science writers, and they had been promulgated by the "old" conservation societies and critical scientists and science students in more or less established ways. It was, however, only when the three dimensions were combined, in the early 1970s, in a new set of organizations by particular "movement intellectuals" that environmentalism could grow into a social movement.

Our three dimensions capture only a part of the environmental movement's cognitive praxis, but they seem to capture most of what is essential to understand both the specificity of the environmental movement as well as its connections to the other social movements around at the same time. The environmental movement had, and in some countries still has, its own identity, but that identity formed part of a larger or at least broader period of social movement activity, interconnecting in a variety of ways with other particular movements of the 1970s and 1980s. Indeed, the ambition to combine particular "single-issue" interests in one political force, while retaining autonomy or specificity, seems to be a defining characteristic of the new social movements of our times. The identity of the new environmental movement or women's movement is part of a broader social struggle, but each movenent also involves a specific struggle around specific issues. By dividing cognitive praxis into various component parts, we try to capture both the general and the specific in the cognitive identity of a social movement.

We do not mean to suggest that the emergence or political influence of environmentalism, or any other social movement, can be explained solely on the basis of its cognitive praxis. The strength of environmentalism as a social movement has been due to particular economic and political conditions in particular countries. Environmentalism has developed in different countries in different ways depending on the political culture and the "opportunity structures" that have been available (Kitschelt 1986; Rudig 1988). But, in just about every country, an environmental movement has emerged during the 1970s and 1980s as an active political force. Green ideas have begun to spread into corporations as well as government bureaucracies and parliaments. An evaluation of those ideas is impossible, we contend, without understanding the cognitive development of the movement that spawned them.

In Sweden, the influence of the established political culture was extremely strong, and a particular movement identity had difficulty in forming itself (Jamison 1987); evironmentalism was largely incorporated into the established institutions. By contrast, in Denmark and the Netherlands the cognitive praxis of the new environmental movement could continue to develop in its own space throughout the 1970s and even beyond. Our argument is that environmentalism can be called a social movement only to the extent that the three "knowledge interests" were combined into an active integrative force – into a living cognitive praxis – among environmental activists. Where they split apart or were incorporated into the established political culture, as in Sweden, environmentalism scarcely existed as a social movement, that is, as a relatively autonomous public space of its own. Where there were alternative political traditions and opportunity structures, as in Denmark and the Netherlands, environmentalism continued to exist as a social movement; interestingly enough, in those countries where the movements have been strong, green parliamentary parties have been relatively weak.

## From knowledge interests to cognitive praxis

The dimensions of cognitive praxis are our own translation of the "knowledge constituting interests" that Jürgen Habermas discussed in the 1960s (Habermas 1972). When we initiated our research on environmentalism we transformed the philosophical or epistemological categories discussed by Habermas into operational categories of "knowledge interests" that could be seen as central to the historical project of actual social movements. Our ambition was to contextualize Habermas's conceptualization, to develop categories that could serve as a set of research variables. We transformed the ahistorical, or transcendental, concepts of Habermas into historical terms. The interests that he imputed onto the human species, that he considered constitutive of human knowledge, were transformed into specifiable interests or types of knowledge that particular movements could be seen to have articulated. We thus set out to identify the cosmological, technological, and organizational knowledge interests in the contemporary environmental movements.

It is first and foremost through its cosmology, its worldview, that a social movement articulates its historical meaning. The cosmological dimension represents the common worldview assumptions that give a social movement its utopian mission, or, to speak with Habermas, that represent its emancipatory aims. But unlike Habermas's emancipatory interest, our cosmological dimension can be found in specific texts, in movement documents, programs, books, articles, etc. In short, it can be "read", that is, reconstructed from really existing materials.

Similarly, our technological dimension is a translation, or operationalization, of Habermas's technical-practical interest. Where Habermas imputes that interest to all technological knowledge as a kind of transcendental goal, we want to be able to locate it in particular movements, that is to identify the specific technological issues that particular movements develop around. What kind of technology do they propagate and develop? What kind of criticisms do they direct against established patterns of technological development? More generally, what specific concerns, what specific issues, do they articulate in their practical activity? Again, what distinguishes our dimension from Habermas's is the "readability" of our concept, the fact that it can be located in specific movement texts and contexts.

Finally, our third dimension, the organizational, is an attempt to operationalize the third knowledge-constituting interest of Habermas, to which he has come to devote ever more attention in recent years, namely the communicative interest, originally claimed to be constitutive of the social sciences. For us, all movements have a particular organizational paradigm, which means that they have both ideals and modes of organizing the production and, even more importantly perhaps, the dissemination of knowledge. The organizational dimension is thus the way in which movements get their message across, and the organizational forms within which their cognitive praxis unfolds.

As we used them in our research, the dimensions of knowledge interest came to take on a deeper meaning. We came to see them not merely as research variables, as categories for empirical research, but as the cornerstones of a movement identity. As we examined the histories of the environmental movements in Sweden, Denmark, and the Netherlands, we realized that, particularly during the second half of the 1970s, the dimensions were integrated into a living active force, they fed on each other, the worldview assumptions providing technical criteria for a range of oppositional activities carried out in new organizational forms. In the course of the 1980s, we saw an increasing differentiation of the dimensions, as the ecological philosophers became socially accepted as legitimate cultural and political figures, and the alternative technologists formed companies and consulting firms to market their new environmental products. What had been an integrated process of social learning in the heat of antinuclear opposition in the late 1970s, when environmentalism had been viewed as one of the"new social movements," had by the late 1980s largely fragmented into more or less separate and quasi-professional activities. We thus translated our descriptive categories of knowledge interest into the concept of cognitive praxis. As dimensions of cognitive praxis, cosmology, technique, and organization become components of a social activity rather than aspects of thought. They become dimensions of a living movement rather than disembodied forms of consciousness.

These dimensions thus serve as an analytical framework: they provide the categories within which a movement's cognitive identity can be conceptualized. Our original term, knowledge interests, was valuable in our empirical investigation, in providing a structure for our searching through movement documents and interviewing activists. The dimensions of knowledge interest offer a skeletal or structural concept of a movement that can then be embodied as the researcher reconstructs the three dimensions of a movement's cognitive praxis. As the research proceeds, the researcher becomes better able to clarify both the contents and the dynamic trajectories of the movement being studied, as our studies of environmentalism show. The following discussion, drawn from that research, is meant to illustrate how the three dimensions could be identified in the case of the environmental movement. We will try to indicate how cognitive praxis can be seen as a process of integrating different sources of cognitive influences into a movement identity. We will then try to show how our cognitive approach can be applied to other social movements, in particular the working-class movements of the nineteenth century and the student movements of the 1960s.

## The cosmological dimension

The cosmological dimension consists of the worldview assumptions, the attitudes to nature and society, and most especially of their interrelationships, which have been associated with the new environmentalist consciousness (cf. Pepper 1984). Central here are the concepts of ecology – ecosystem, dynamic balance, states of equilibrium, niche, network, etc. – which were adopted by environmental activists in the late 1960s and early 1970s as a defining part of their movement identity. Systems ecology was not created by the environmental movement, but it was certainly influential in the formation of the environmental movement's cognitive praxis. Indeed, what the environmental movement contributed was an audience, and a potential social carrier for the ideas that had been developing within ecological science. In the words of Dorothy Nelkin, "The environmental movement brought the discipline of ecology into public view. Once perceived as a useful resource, public demands have affected many aspects of the discipline and popular definitions of 'ecology' contributed to problems of defining it as a bounded scientific field" (Nelkin 1977: 78).

But the movement did more than merely support a discipline on the rise, or spread a set of ideas developed elsewhere. Environmentalism as a social movement actually embodied the ideas of systems ecology, and this in two main ways. First, the environmental groups and the new environmental activists protesting particular cases of pollution or resource exploitation were translating scientific ideas into social action. They acted on ideas that had emerged out of studying processes in nature and transformed those natural concepts into social ones. Cosmology formation in this regard is thus a kind of translation process, translating terms from an internal scientific discourse to public space, to social and political action. What was learned from nature was applied to society: ecological theory conceptualized certain fundamental processes at work in the natural world, processes between individual species and their environments, and those conceptualizations were taken by the environmental movement as social precepts, as the rudiments of social theory. "An ecological perspective grew from the popularization of knowledge about natural processes," Samuel Hays has written. "These were ideas significant to the study of ecology, but selected and modified by popular experience rather than as a result of formal study" (Hays 1987: 27).

Already in the 1940s Aldo Leopold was writing about ecological ethics, but he was still writing within a conservation discourse. His ecology was concerned with social precepts for ensuring wilderness and the preservation of species. With Rachel Carson (1962) and then Barry Commoner (1966, 1972), Murray Bookchin (1971), Edward Goldsmith (in *The Ecologist*, 1972), and a host of others writing in the late 1960s and early 1970s, ecology was transformed into a kind of social philosophy. Commoner's *The Closing Circle* and Goldsmith's *Blueprint for Survival* were translations of ecological theory to political beliefs, to social theory; they were attempts to develop a social ecology rather than a natural one.

As a break with the old conservationism which separated nature from society and acted on a continued separation – that is what wilderness preservation is ultimately all about – the environmental movement presupposed an ecological society, and by presupposing it, by conceptualizing it, it acted to achieve it. In this sense, the ecological cosmology is a form of what Karl Mannheim called a utopia, in that it "orients conduct towards elements which the situation, in so far as it is realized at the time, does not contain" (Mannheim 1948: 176). The ecological worldview that has now spawned institutes of human and social ecology around the world as well as made inroads into both natural and social science disciplines is something different from ecological science. It is the translation of a scientific paradigm, that is, of ecosystem ecology, to societal terms. Writing at the time, the journalist James Ridgeway wrote, "Ecology became a popular issue during the early spring of 1970 because it momentarily offered the prospects of a new politics, a new set of symbols with which to rework the social order" (Ridgeway 1970: 13).

During the 1960s, the ecological consciousness emerged as a critique of the modern industrial state and its destruction of the natural environment. It emerged, as do most social movements, as a body of reaction or protest; it was transformed into a movement when new organizations developed and when the environmental problems could be understood within a new kind of conceptual framework provided by systems ecology. This movement building owed, as we shall see in the final section of this chapter, a great deal to the general political climate, and to the "liberatory" project of the student movement. Within that all-encompassing but extremely fleeting spirit of liberation, the environmental movement carved out its own somewhat more specialized cognitive space.

The political message of ecology, which Ridgeway at its formation in 1970 criticized for being too "liberal," developed in the following decade into a variety of different directions. At its core, according to Stephen Cotgrove, was an alternative social paradigm, an alternative program for social development that based itself on certain social and political applications of ecological concepts (Cotgrove 1982). And all the deep and shallow, the radical and reformist, the fundamental and the simpleminded, the green and the red versions of the ecological worldview that have followed on its emergence have all grown out of that alternative environmental paradigm.

The environmental movement embodied the concepts of ecology by contextualizing and politicizing them,but also by internalizing them. The ecologist as a scientist can only study natural processes; indeed scientific legitimation is based on the objective distance that the ecologist is able to establish between him/herself and the objects of study. An ecologist can thus develop ecological theory, but he steps outside of science if he attempts to develop ecological philosophy or, for that matter, ecological politics. It was the environmental movement that transformed a scientific theory into a way of life, but even more perhaps into a set of beliefs. The movement provided, we might say, the social context for a new kind of knowledge to be practiced.

There was no talk, before the environmental movement began to put its ecological cosmology into practice, of ecological living or ecological lifestyles or even ecological poetry. The movement made the space for those types of knowledge and experience to be able to emerge. Even an ecological theology and philosophy, such as the systems proposed by the Danish priest Ole Jensen or the Norwegian philosopher Arne Naess grew out of the movement. Both developed their own innovations in their professional discourses on the basis of experiences derived from movement praxis. For Naess, the experience of participating in the protests against hydroelectric power in Norway even led to a formal withdrawal from the academic environment (Eyerman 1983).

In both cases, and in the case of countless other poets, artists, teachers, as well as scientists, the movement created the cosmology, the worldview that, in turn, formed the assumptions through which new thoughts were thought in a variety of disciplines and areas of knowledge. Indeed, it has been suggested that it was largely through the space created by the environmental movement that cosmology itself was rediscovered, and that worldview assumptions were taken up for discussion. For Stephen Toulmin, the environmental movement and the questions it raised marked a "return to cosmology" after a long period of noncosmological hegemony (Toulmin 1982).

Throughout the 1970s an ecological worldview formed an important part of the shared belief system of the environmental movement. It served as a kind of common denominator – and still does for many environmental activists – but it was seldom discussed or articulated within the movement in a formalized or systematic way. It was taken for granted as a characteristic element of the environmentalist identity. An ecological perspective or paradigm provided a set of assumptions that served as ideals rather than ideology. It existed as phrases – harmony with nature, diversity gives stability, nature knows best, limits to growth – rather than programs, beliefs rather than systematic theory. It often came out better in illustrations, in cartoons, showing how everything is related to every-thing else, or how unlimited growth was unnatural, rather than in worked-out philosophy. The graphics of M. C. Escher or the car-toons of Ron Cobb encapsulated the ecological worldview as much as the writings of Commoner, Goldsmith, or Naess.

There were even explicit attempts to formulate the ecological vision in literary form. Ernest Callenbach's *Ecotopia*, written in 1975, and Marge Piercy's *Woman on the Edge of Time*, written in 1976, both attempted to portray the ecological social vision, the ecological utopia as a living reality. Nor was ecologism as utopian mentality only presented in literary form; European social ecology, as expressed, for instance, in the writings of André Gorz (1982) and Rudolf Bahro (1984) was largely responsible for resuscitating utopian theory as a mode of political discourse, In many countries, the old utopian classics were republished, and authors like William Morris and Charles Fourier were rediscovered, largely under the influence of the environmental movement.

Central to both the artists and the theorists was the notion of system, of the whole being more than the sum of its parts, of intricate interconnections among species and between individuals and their environments. The ecological worldview was first and foremost a re-cognition of system, but also a rediscovery of the omnipresence of systemic interconnections in all kinds of relation-ships, both within nature, within societies, as well as between nature and society.

The worldview, or cosmological dimension, is fundamental to the cognitive identity of the environmental movement, but as the movement developed, the ecological worldview came under attack, or rather it was forced to define itself in political-strategic terms, and in the process the movement fragmented. There were those who attempted to combine ecology with socialism or Marxism, and throughout the industrialized world groups were formed, confer-ences were held, journals published, and treatises written (for a recent attempt, see Ryle 1988). And there were those who sought to link the interests of the ecology movement with feminism and with pacifism, and those who sought to incorporate an ecological worldview into more established political parties or traditions. In short, as the movement grew in social importance, primarily through the struggles over nuclear energy in the late 1970s, the ecological worldview split apart in a number of different directions.

And as it diffused, it tended also in many countries to leave the space of the movement behind.

In countries like Sweden and Britain with strong working-class traditions, the ecological perspective was perhaps more successfully incorporated into the parties and organizations of the "old" social movements than in countries, like the US, where socialist traditions are weak. There was also an incorporation into established academic traditions, as environmental history, environmental philosophy, and environmental ethics emerged as new specialties in universities and professional societies.

## The technological and organizational dimensions

Ecological philosophy, however, was not alone in representing the cognitive identity of the environmental movement. Even more important in many contexts was the practical, or what we have called the technological, dimension of knowledge interest. If ecology formed the terms of the discourse for the movement, it was the critique of modern chemical and nuclear technologies that gave the discourse its substance. What the movement talked about was the pollution of the environment, the deterioration of the environment, the dangers to human health and to global survival caused by the use of particular technologies. The technological dimension provides the specifics of the environmental movement's cognitive praxis, and for a time the particular objects of critique were selected in accordance with an ecological worldview. Even more importantly, perhaps, was that for a time there was a conscious search within the movement for alternative technologies: indeed, the articulation of alternative technology in agriculture, energy, medicine, even industrial production formed a central component of the identity of the environmental movement in many countries. Particularly in countries like Denmark and Holland, where craftsmanship has long been central to national autonomy and identity, environmental technology came to occupy a pride of place in the making of the environmental movement. The Danish windmills and the Dutch appropriate technology projects in the third world grew out of but were also formative influences on the development of environmentalism. The idea of ecological or clean technology – an idea whose time seems to have come in many engineering circles, a new technological paradigm or design principle – together with many of its applications, is a product of the environmental movement.

Again, the early 1970s were a period when books were written, groups were formed, workshops and demonstration projects were developed, and not least, popular technical courses and seminars were held. Ivan Illich (1973) wrote about "tools for conviviality," David Dickson (1974) wrote about utopian technology, and E. F. Schumacher (1973) told us that small is beautiful, and thousands of grassroots engineers, movement activists, tried to act on their precepts, creating the vision of an alternative technology as an embodiment of the environmental movement's cognitive praxis. (The best contemporary survey remains Boyle and Harper 1976.) Like its cosmological counterpoint, alternative technology represented the utopian mentality – but at a practical level. David Dickson called the alternative products and processes he surveyed in 1974 "utopian technology," not, he wrote "to imply that the tools and machines described are impracticable, but to indicate that their introduction in a significant scale would be virtually impossible within the existing structure of society" (Dickson 1974: 99). Many of us, maybe even most of us, failed at our amateur technological activity, but some survived and yet interestingly enough the survivors, much like the surviving ecological philosophers, have tended to leave the movement behind them. Instead, they have become established entrepreneurs, or teachers of engineering or professional technologists, developing their "biotechnology" or ecological technology in more or less established institutional settings. What was once utopian practice has become commercial business. Such is the nature of a social movement. It creates a space for new occupational activities to emerge.

Between the theory and the practice, the cosmological and the technological dimensions, there is the organizational dimension. In the environmental movement, the identity also included a critique of elitism, a challenge to the established scientific and intellectual order. Knowledge, the environmental movement contended, should serve the people. Here of course, the identity of the environmental movement, with its active dissemination of scientific information, its popularization of ecology and its demands for relevant interdisciplinary environmental education, merged with the identities of the other new social movements. Indeed, to a large extent, the organizational dimension of the environmental movement's cognitive praxis was a legacy of the student movement of the 1960s, providing a kind of specialization, along with the women's movement and later the peace movement, of what was a more diffuse and all-encompassing emancipatory project in the 1960s. Although the actual trajectories of environmentalism differed from country to country, all owed something to the space opened up by the student movement or the "new left," an interest in a knowledge for the people that led to organizational innovations such as the Dutch science shops and to visions of, and experiments in, democratic science and participatory science policy, which were outgrowths of the anti-elitism of the 1960s.

Environmentalism thus had many "sources," There was the scientific input, the concepts of systems ecology that had been developing among scientists for half a century. The environmental movement took that language and its assumptions about natural processes and translated them into social terms, into political action. Ecology was transformed by the environmental movement into a social ecology, an ecological social philosophy, and as such it has become an important ingredient in new political programs as well as theories in several social sciences. There was the material or technological input, the visible destruction of the environment brought about by chemical industries, polluting automobiles, and wasteful industrial production processes, as well as the potential risks inherent in nuclear power plants. The environmental movement was formed as a critique of those technologies and even more of the technological paradigm or system on which they were based. And finally there was the movement input, the influence from the participatory fervor, the rediscovery of democracy, that was the 1960s. The environmental movement focused that interest in participation into particular directions.

From our perspective, what made environmentalism into a social movement was its combination of the three dimensions into a core identity. As a movement it carved out a new conceptual space, giving the "environment" and ecology political and economic significance that, in the course of the 1980s, have affected the political cultures of almost every nation. The antinuclear movement of the 1970s combined the three dimensions of cognitive praxis into a process of social learning that led to the more formalized Green parties of the 1980s. Environmentalism as a social movement combined an ecological worldview and a vision of an alternative technology with an interest in participatory decision-making born out of the 1960s. It didn't last very long as a social movement in most countries, but it would be hard to find a country where it didn't exist at all.

In the following chapter, we will return to the environmental movement and identify the types of intellectuals who have articulated the movement's cognitive identity. But now let us turn to another kind of social movement and attempt to indicate the potential generalizability of our concepts. Is a cognitive approach a meaningful way to "read" social movements other than environmentalism?

## The nineteenth-century social movements as cognitive praxis

Much of the recent sociolological discussion about social movements has been concerned with the relationship between the new and the old movements of the nineteenth century. Some contend that the new movements are to be distinguished from the old because of their specificity, and even more for their classlessness (Olofsson 1987). This means that the new social movements of our time are not so much struggling for power as for autonomy, not seeking political results as much as "cultural" or sociocultural change (Melucci 1988). There is, many claim, a fundamental difference between the new social movements with their partial goals and the old social movements of the working class (Offe 1985).

An opposing school of thought seeks to understand the new movements in terms of the old, either in class terms or in terms of some kind of cyclical theory of history. The new social movements are thereby seen as signalling the emergence of new class actors – a professional class, a middle class, a managerial class, or a combination thereof (Kriesi 1989; Gouldner 1979). Environmental activism has been depicted by many sociologists and by many representatives of the "old" social movements as a kind of middle-class activism, as have many forms of feminism and peace activism. The point here is not that the new social movements are similar to the old; rather, the new movements are seen as antagonistic to the old, the implicit or explicit class enemies of the working class. Of course, the more sophisticated analysts look for points of possible alliance or convergence between the new and the old, but most class-oriented analyses tend to downplay the historical importance of the new movements, since they do not represent a class that has become embroiled in what Alain Touraine calls the "struggle for historicity" (Touraine 1981).

The cyclical explanations draw a somewhat different set of distinctions between the old and the new social movements. In this perspective, social movements are seen as being linked to particular historical cycles: business cycles, generational cycles, "long waves" of economic development, etc. (Jamison 1988; Frank and Fuentes 1988). Movements are themselves seen as cyclical, having their own lifecycles and their own internal dynamics, related to, but not necessarily identical with, the larger historical cycles of the political or economic spheres. The new movements are thus similar to the old in that they are both responses to "crisis" or critical, declining conjunctures in a business or political cycle. The movements of our time and the movements of the nineteenth century can be seen as fundamentally similar kinds of social phenomena, that is, responses to crisis.

From there, the various explanations differ as to just what social movements stand for. Most functionalists see movements as symptoms of crisis, or of systemic disfunction, which fade away as the crisis is resolved (Smelser 1962). Others see movements as initiators of change, by identifying problems that need to be dealt with and even taking part in the problem solution process (Banks 1972; Friberg and Galtung 1984). For our purposes, cyclical theories are important for indicating continuities between the new social movements and the old ones of the nineteenth century. What is crucial is that social movements are seen as processes, and not as things-in-themselves, as historical moments rather than ahistorical organizations. It is in that spirit that we want to examine some of the cognitive similarities between the old and the new social movements. In chapter 6, we will discuss some of the crucial contextual differences.

The social movements of the nineteenth century are usually conceived as responses to broader socioeconomic development processes. For many if not most analysts, both historians and sociologists, the nineteenth century movements have generally been explained as reactions to the coming of industrialization. Views differ as to what it is about industrialization that leads to the emergence of social movements: for Smelser, it was the "structural strain"; for Thompson it was the destruction of old values and relationships that inspired the formation of new ones, and indeed the making of a working class (Thompson 1966). Others, like

Maxine Berg (1880) and David Noble (1983), have pointed to the scientific and technological roots of the working-class movements, seeing them as responses to the mechanization of production, while many others have characterized the nineteenth-century movements as reactions to the discipline and order of the factory system with its regimentation of daily life.

Our ambition is not primarily to challenge any of these inter-pretations. Rather, we want to shift the focus of attention from response to creation, from seeing movements as socioeconomic reactors to seeing them as cognitive actors. For us, the movements of the nineteenth-century are not primarily significant as responses to social change, but as (epistemological) creators of industrial society. By exploring the cognitive praxis of the nineteenth-century movements, we hope to indicate something of their historically constructive role. For it is our contention that like the new social movements, of which environmentalism has served as our illustra-tive example, the old movements also provided space for new thought to emerge, and indirectly for new institutions, vocations, and scientific theories.

We can begin by dividing up the movements of the nineteenth-century into a first and a second wave. Even a cursory reading of nine-teenth-century history shows that the mid-century – Hobsbawm's "age of capital" – is a period of retrenchment for the industrial capitalists which separates two rather distinct periods of working-class mobilization in most European countries. The 1850s and 1860s are a time of institution building and capitalist expansion when social movements are in decline. It is in the periods of crisis and depression, especially in the 1830s and the 1880s that movements are on the rise, forming new organizations, mounting political cam-paigns, and, in our terms, articulating their cognitive praxis. By seeking to characterize the dimensions of that praxis, we may better understand just what those movements actually represented.

We need to tread cautiously here, and not read our contem-porary concerns into the historical past. For these were, as E. P. Thompson has argued perhaps more convincingly than anyone else, historical phemomena, and they involved real people in specific locations. We should be careful about trying to find a larger mean-ing in what they did. But obviously there was a larger meaning: without the making of the working class in England, for in-stance, with its distinct class consciousness or its distinct cognitive identity, English society would certainly have developed differently. The difficulty, however, is in indicating the precise role that the movement played.

This is where our three dimensions of cognitive praxis can be especially fruitful to use as analytical instruments. But we must qualify them at the outset, or rather we must contextualize them if they are to be usable in the nineteenth century. We are obliged not merely to look for a distinct cognitive praxis in specific movements but we need to place those movements in national, or cultural context. Thus the worldview dimension, the cosmology, of the English movements can be expected to differ from that of the French or the German. Similarly the specifics of the movements' cognitive praxis, the technological dimension, should differ as well. Not all countries developed their technology at the same time in the same way. What we want to stress, however, is for all the differences, due to context and level of development and political traditions, there were certain significant commonalities, as well. Let us briefly describe them.

First of all, there was a common challenge or questioning of traditional beliefs about nature and about society. As opposed to the religious or idealized views of the feudal past, the social movements of the nineteenth century identified with the material and, even more, the empirical approaches to understanding natural phenomena that had been developed by the experimental philosophers. Experimental science had itself been an outgrowth of the social movements of the seventeeth century, and it had served as a source of inspiration for the revolutions of the late eighteenth century. By the early nineteenth century, experimental science had become institutionalized in most European countries, and its world-view had come to form part of the new industrial ideology. What the social movements did was develop a new social identity on the basis of this empirical and material worldview.

As with contemporary movements, the early working-class movement translated scientific philosophy into social philosophy. In England Robert Owen was perhaps the main leader of a broad movement that sought to apply Baconian methods to society; and in France, the utopian theories of Saint-Simon and Charles Fourier also conceptualized society as a space for social experimentation. For most people, the movements of the early nineteenth century are mostly known through the theories of these "utopian socialists," as they were labeled by Friedrich Engels towards the end of the century, when he was trying to distinguish his own scientific socialism from the theories of his predecessors. But this is to draw a false dichotomy between science and utopia. In fact, Owen, Saint-Simon, and Fourier were extremely scientific. Their project, as was that of the period of social movement within which they wrote, was to broaden science, to apply the methods and the very essence of experimental science to society. The famous triumvirate, which actually represented rather different interest groups, was only the most formalized part of a movement cognitive praxis. What informed that praxis was a belief in social experimentation, and what the movement articulated was thus the very idea of social sciencing. It is no accident that the young Engels's investigation of the conditions of the working class in Manchester in 1844 has been called the first example of empirical social science; nor should it surprise us that Owenist teachers in movement schools were the first to develop a labor theory of value. The first political economists sociologists, and social psychologists were all contemporary with the social movement of the 1830s and 1840s.

The important thing is not to give the early nineteenth-century social movements "credit" for creating one or another field of social science, although their role was obviously significant. Rather, our aim is to indicate that the social movements opened up a cognitive space that made social science possible. Participants in the social movement – such as the Owenists and the Chartists in England and the followers of Proudhon and Cabet in France – took the ideas of the academic political economists and social philosophers and acted on them; in their cognitive praxis, they embodied a social sciencing, a socially experimental activity, which later came to be professionalized by Mill and others in the "discipline" of political economy.

Owen and Fourier did not merely translate scientific materialism or empirical philosophy to social relations; their social cosmology was also envisioning, or what is usually referred to as utopian. They specified the contours of the desirable, they articulated a vision of a future classless society. The limitations of Owen's vision, in particular the overly optimistic view of how environmental changes could alter human behavior, need not concern us. Here as elsewhere in the writings of the early nineteenth-century social activists are found sources of inspiration for what would later become scientific disciplines: social psychology, industrial organization, organizational theory. What Owen, Fourier, Proudhon, and a host of others actually established was something far more essential than specific social science approaches. In their writings, and even more perhaps in their actual praxis they created a new set of beliefs about how social relationships should be constructed, and they articulated a socialist worldview in the sense that they specified how assumptions of equality and equitable distribution of social resources could form the basis for a society. Socialism as a belief system or social cosmology was central to the cognitive identity of the social movement of the 1830s and 1840s. What later became separated into political activity on the one hand and cultural/intellectual discourse on the other was, in this brief period, combined in an all-encompassing social movement (Thompson 1966).

The specific contents of that identity differed from country to country. The importance of the practical, or technological, dimension was largely dependent on how strong the impact of the new-mechanical instruments of production had been in the particular context. In England, protests against textile and agricultural machinery were particularly intense; the Luddite revolts in the 1810s were formative influences on the social movements of the early nineteenth century. Owenism propagated an alternative technological vision, and in the Owenite communities, machines were largely rejected in favor of artisan production. In other contexts, machines were not opposed directly, but it was the misuse of the machine, its negative social and human consequences that were criticized. In all places, however, the social movement of the 1830s asserted the value of the artisan, the skilled worker. Indeed, to a large extent, the movements consisted of skilled workers banding together to defend their interests. Their ambition was for the new experimental philosophy or natural science to be of benefit for them, and in their workshops they experimented with new tools of agricultural and industrial production that had less deleterious human consequences. This was the period not so much of resistance to the machine as of cultural assimilation and popularization. The social movements criticized the way technology was used to dominate workers and to take skill away from individual workers, but they also popularized technology by establishing institutes and schools and by struggling for general public education.

In general terms, we might say that the problem was not technology itself so much as the organizing principle of technology, what Christopher Freeman has called the dominant techno-economic paradigm (in Dosi et al., 1988). As Thompson put it, "What was at issue was not so much the machine as the profit-motive" (Thompson 1966: 804). In the classical industrial revolution, machinery had been applied haphazardly within the individual factory. The machines had been developed unsystematically, solving particular problems in particular production processes. The social movements that arose as the first industrial revolution was moving into a period of decline opposed this unsystematic type of technology. They pointed to the social consequences, the disorientation, the unhealthy working conditions, the lack of learning by doing. Some skilled workers experimented with the new machines, and sought to deal with some of the unintended consequences. Others looked for new applications of the new machines, and still others explored the underlying principles of mechanical production. It would be claiming too much to suggest that the social movements were in some way responsible for the articulation of a new techno-economic paradigm. But there should be no doubt that the critical space opened up by the movement encouraged the technically minded to find ways to solve the problems that the movement identified. And when it did emerge, the new paradigm of systematized technical development did owe some of its inspiration to the technical ideas generated within the movement. The very professionalization of the civil engineer and the creation of technological universities was, to a large extent, a response to the criticisms that the social movements had levelled against the anarchic technical development process. That technological development had unintended side effects that needed to be dealt with, and that the industrial society necessitated infrastructural engineering – for communication, transportation, sewage disposal, public health, etc. – was an idea that grew out of the cognitive praxis of the early nineteenth-century social movements.

Their historical project was most clearly articulated at perhaps above all else an organizational level, an attempt to put the new instruments of production to use in a cooperative way. What was promulgated was not a rejection of industrialization but an ambition to control industrialization in appropriate organizational structures. The social movements of the 1830s and 1840s experimented actively with social organization through the establishment of experimental communities, particularly in North America, the development of alternative technology workshops, the creation of new forms of schooling and education. The assertion of popular sovereignty, an assertion that had begun to be expressed already in the eighteenth-century revolutions, was applied by the social movements to knowledge production and dissemination. As such, the movements, with different intensity in different countries, opened up a space that was subsequently filled by the general system of public education and publicly sponsored research and development. More specifically perhaps, the social movements, by organizing knowledge production and dissemination in cooperative ways, transformed knowledge itself, which had previously been considered the result of individual acts of genius, into a socially constituted activity.

As the movement space came to be filled with new state and privately supported institutions, however, the original utopian ambition – which has been characterized by Jos Kingston as an ambition for "self-education" – also tended to fade away. "Without the deadening effect of a state education system designed to suppress any tendency towards fundamental questioning," Kingston wrote in the mid-1970s, "a substantial number of working people possessed a tremendous appetite for discovery, and an untrammeled, free-ranging way of looking at the world. Owenite socialism, and generally, the radicalism of the early nineteenth century, had about it a vitality, a contagious hopefulness and a deep sense of the rightness of the cause" (Kingston 1976: 246).

What E. P. Thompson has called "perhaps the most distinguished popular culture England has known" with its "more earnest attempts to pioneer new forms of community life than any in our history" (Thompson 1966: 831, 804) was, however, only a brief period of time, a short social movement. In mid-century, as the movements weakened in most countries, their cognitive praxis was disembodied and their historical project came to be fragmented. The more radical ambitions were discarded, the more moderate ones incorporated into the institutional structure of the new industrial societies. Technical education, for instance, was greatly expanded, and some farsighted capitalists even established research laboratories. Also significant was the new "cooperation" among entrepreneurs, as they established jointstock companies and began the process of incorporating their individual factories into larger units. This was particularly essential for the major projects of the period, the construction of railroads and other transportation and communication facilities and the development of machine-building industries and large-scale manufacture.

These changes in the institutional infrastructure of industrial society affected the identity of the social movement which rose to prominence in the 1870s and 1880s. The business cycle had once again entered a period of decline and critical voices could once again mobilize the population for protest activity. The late 1870s and 1880s witnessed a wave of strikes and demonstrations, and attempts in most industrial countries to form working-class organizations, labor unions. This was the time of the Second International, and, for many countries, the social movements that developed sought to base themselves on a more "scientific" theory such as the one developed by Karl Marx.

The scientific ambition meant several things for the cognitive praxis of the social movements of the 1870s and onward. On the one hand, it meant a critical distancing from the earlier movements. Now, in many countries, working-class leaders were drawn from the bourgeoisie, from professional intellectuals, even academics. A kind of professionalism entered into the working-class or socialist movements, even though certain spokesmen, such as the Russian anarchist Mikhail Bakunin, strongly criticized this elitist tendency (Gouldner 1985). Secondly, the scientific ambition meant that, for many, the more visionary aspects of socialist thought were rejected. As Friedrich Engels put it, socialism had moved from a utopian to a scientific stage, corresponding to transformations in the material base of society. Utopianism, for the scientific socialist, belonged to a preindustrial past. This meant that science often degenerated into a kind of scientism, that is an unquestioning belief or faith in the truths of natural science (Kolakowski 1978).

The cosmology of the late nineteenth-century movements was thus a kind of social positivism. The social movements embodied a cosmology of evolutionary fatalism, by which the socialist future of society was largely taken for granted. Capitalism, it was assumed by many, basing themselves on the popular versions of Marxian theory that were widely disseminated at this time, was seen as leading almost inevitably to socialism, and thus utopian thinking had to be replaced by planning and an economic science. The Marxist doctrines, however, which were generally shared by activists throughout the social movements, had different connotations in different countries, and in some countries this inevitability and scientism was relatively weak. In England, for instance, the utopian, even poetic, dimension of socialism remained alive in the writings of William Morris, and elsewhere more spiritual interests and ideas were integrated with socialist thought. It would take us too far afield to explicate the numerous varieties of Marxism: the literature on the subject is vast. For our purposes, it is enough to note that Marxian doctrine – and an ambition to combine "science" with "socialism" – served as an important common denominator in the cognitive praxis of the working-class movements of the late nineteenth century.

The science that was referred to, however, was no longer the experimental philosophy of Boyle and Newton. It was rather the scientific biology of Darwin, in particular his theory of evolution. Social democracy, Hobsbawm has written, "became strongly – and with some of Marx's disciples such as Kautsky excessively – Darwinian" (Hobsbawn 1979: 288). The social movements of the late nineteenth century also acted to translate a scientific theory into social terms; indeed, Marx wanted to dedicate his magnum opus, *Capital*, to Darwin but was politely discouraged. There had of course been theorists of history, but what Marx and his followers supplied was a scientific theory of history. The social movement that they inspired and acted within opened up a space for scientific history. Where the earlier movements had fostered a scientification of society and social relationships, the movements of the late nineteenth century encouraged a scientification of human and social development. Out of it grew new historical subdisciplines: economic history, intellectual history, history of technology, but also new historical approaches within the sciences. The social movements both generalized but also embodied the idea of historical evolution.

On the practical side, the movements were also on the side of science, in particular the new science-based technological fields of organic chemistry and electricity. The movement emerged in reaction to the spreading of industrialization, its diffusion over the continents of Europe and North America. That diffusion had brought with it new organizations, banks and jointstock companies with their industrial barons and their uncouth methods of management and development. And it had taken a heavy toll both on the natural environment and on the ideals of democracy. The social movements that emerged thus challenged the ugliness, the destruction, the authoritarian character of technological and industrial development. In the new science-based technologies of electricity and chemistry, movement spokesmen envisioned a new kind of socialist technological society – the mass organized production facilities of Edward Bellamy's *Looking Backward* or the decentralized aesthetic modernity of William Morris. Contemporary with the social movements came the emergence of science fiction, that popular form of utopian writing that envisioned a new world based on science, the not yet discovered. Jules Verne wrote in a space, a futuristic, scientistic space, that had been carved out by the social movement: just as history moved inevitably toward socialism, so science moved inevitably toward conquering the universe.

As its organizational contribution, the social movement of the late nineteenth century created the modern labor union and the modern political party. Representation of the working class had to be formalized if it was to be effective. The social democratic parties which later split among communists and social democrats all grew out of the social movement of strikes and worker demonstrations. Indeed, the creation of the party was in many countries the main activity of the movement. In the face of armed resistance and bourgeois intransigence, the workers fought to create their voice. And all the party programs and slogans, the songs and the poems, the journals and the places to meet were central ingredients of the identity formation of the late nineteenth-century social movements. The point was that organizations should be controlled by members, and even more that even the disadvantaged working class had a right to organize itself and its interests in the parliamentary and broader political system.

Even this brief review brings out, we hope, the constructive role of the "old" social movements in the formation of the modern industrial society, a point to which we shall return in chapter 6. Our ambition has not been to give a comprehensive history of the working-class movements; we have rather wanted to show that our conceptual framework can be useful in deepening our understanding of even well-known social movements. By looking for and trying to characterize the dimensions of cognitive praxis in different social movements, we make sources of our contemporary society visible. But even more we see somewhat more clearly what social movements actually represent.

## Reading the new social movements

Let us conclude this chapter by returning to our own research on environmental movements. Our original intention had been to study environmentalism on its own, and compare organizational conglomerations in our three countries. But as the study developed, we realized that a common historical framework was essential if we were to compare developments in three countries. This is not the place to present that scheme, which we have described in detail elsewhere; the point to be made here is that in making a historical scheme we found it impossible to separate environmentalism from other new social movements or from its roots in the 1960s. Reading social movements historically means also identifying their relations to other movements.

In our countries, and almost all other industrial countries as well, for that matter, environmentalism was a product of the 1960s. For developing countries, the situation is more complicated, as environmentalism was also a product of "knowledge transfer," that is an import from the West as well as something homegrown. For industrialized countries, however, environmentalism was one of the unintended results of the 1960s, even though its development into a social movement differed from country to country.

What all industrial countries seem to have gone through is a period of revolt in the 1960s. It was primarily a student movement, and the main focus was on the war in Vietnam, although the "imagination" of the new left, as it has been called, was certainly more all-encompassing (Katsiaficas 1987). The new left had its roots in the enormous expansion of the tertiary sector, and within it the system of higher education, in the two decades following the end of the Second World War. The postwar techno-economic paradigm was excessively science-based; this was the age of Big Science, epitomized by nuclear energy, industrial automation, and petrochemical products. And the science-based firms required highly skilled workers with college educations. Universities were thus transformed into teaching factories, and the knowledge that was transmitted and produced was itself transformed into marketable commodities. As a capsule characterization, the student movement of the 1960s can be seen as an international revolt against these developments, a massive cry of outrage against the modern scientific-technological state.

The student movement was first and foremost a defense of freedom: freedom of speech, freedom of research, freedom of expression, freedom of personal career choice. It was a "great refusal" to participate in the use of science and technology – and all knowledge – in the corporate system, and, more precisely, in the "military-industrial complex" (Marcuse 1969). The movement experimented with new forms of relevant education, inventing the teach-in, the counter course, the free school, the concerned professional academic. The student movement practiced its cognition more than articulating it; it was in what we would call its organizational dimension that the student movement defined its movement place. In the 1960s, the new processes of social learning that have become so central to the new social movements first emerged. The affinity group, the national network, the underground of alternative media, and the creative use of electronic media are all products of the student movement.

In our terms, the 1960s represented the first phase of the new social movements, a period of awakening after the big sleep of postwar prosperity. Out of apathy arose a new generation of social actors, who created a new movement; more than anything else, the 1960s stood for a re-cognition of direct democracy. Students organized themselves for a "democratic society" in the US and Germany, and their actions sought to rediscover what democratic behavior was all about. Industrial society had become in the eyes of many students a bureaucratic, mass society without ideology or any coherent value system. Like the beat generation before them, the students sought escape, color, adventure; but they also sought meaning and expressed solidarity with their own racially oppressed countrymen and peoples of the third world. Out of apathy arose a generation that took to the streets in the name of a vague, all-encompassing liberation. In the words of Todd Gitlin, the movement in the US was a "fusion of collective will and moral style. The movement didn't simply demand, it did. By taking action, not just a position, it affirmed the right to do so; by refusing to defer, it deprived the authorities of authority itself" (Gitlin 1987: 84).

The cosmology of the student movements was given many names, from self-management to people's power to direct action, but what all had in common was a general quest for "liberation" and a general opposition to what Herbert Marcuse in 1964 called "one-dimensional thought." What eventually came to be called the new left stood, like the "old" left before it, for opposition to forces of reaction, but its leftism was new in the sense that it embodied new tactics, new models of social organization, and new sources of inspiration. Particularly important was the influence of the existential philosophy of Camus and Sartre, the humanist psychology of Fromm and Laing, and the third world prophets – Che Guevara, Mao Tse-tung, Franz Fanon, Ho Chi Minh. The student movement translated these influences, and many others, into a kind of liberation cosmology, articulated not so much in any one theory as in massive displays of collective ceremony, from the cultural revolution in China to the Woodstock rock festival in the US. Political and cultural at the same time, the student movement of the 1960s rapidly fragmented into a number of separate movements; in our terms, the student movement of the 1960s was not a social movement in its own right, but was rather a phase in a period of social movement.

Environmental problems were one of the concerns of the 1960s movement, but while the war in Vietnam continued, environmental protest was of secondary importance. Already in the early 1960s, in *Our Synthetic Environment*, Murray Bookchin had combined an ecological critique with a social one, and many antiwar teach-ins included lectures on the ecological damage caused by the American military in Vietnam. But environmentalism, like feminism, remained secondary, even marginal, increasingly dubious to the leaders of the student movement as they grew increasingly infatuated with Marxism and Leninist strategies. By the time the first Earth Day was held in 1970 and new environmental protest groups started to establish themselves throughout the industrialized countries, the student movement had split apart into the range of issue-specific new social movements that still form such a conspicuous part of our collective political culture.

For us, environmentalism and feminism represent a specialization of the all-encompassing new left, a part of a niche-seeking strategy that has continued to characterize the new social movements. The ecological cosmology was one of a number of "limited" liberation cosmologies; and together with feminism epitomized the second, more constructive, phase of social movement which, depending on the country, lasted from the late 1960s on through the 1970s. The new social movements provided specification, a kind of specialization to the rather overextended cosmological ambitions of the 1960s.

Both feminism and environmentalism are inconceivable without the student movement of the 1960s. Their reconceptualizations of nature and gender, and of social relations more generally, were impossible without the articulation of a more fundamental belief in liberation. The 1960s opened the space for the later movements to fill with specific meanings. It provided a number of organizational innovations as well, from the rural commune to the massive demonstration, the rock festival to the encounter group. These were, of course, developed further in the later phases of social movement, but they were created in the 1960s as political phenomena.

From our perspective, distinguishing new social movements from

each other is rather arbitrary. They are, in many respects, component parts of the same social movement, a period of historical
creation that emerged in the 1960s and that had by the end of the
1980s, largely been incorporated into established politics, in the
guise of green parties, mainstream public interest organizations,
women's studies departments, environmental bureaucracies, etc.
Like the old social movements of the nineteenth century, the movement space that was, for a time, so vital and experimental, has
come to be occupied by other social forces, and the cognitive praxis
of the new social movements has been "transferred" into more
established forums: the mass media, the academy, the marketplace,
and, of course, the various national and international agencies that
have been established or reformed in response to the concerns of
the movements. It is not necessary to bemoan the demise of the
movement in order to accept its historical significance; indeed, it
would be our contention that it is only by seeing the movement
historically and dynamically – and by accepting its passing as a
social movement – that its real achievements can be appreciated.
The movement, in a sense, has come and gone, and it ain't left
nothing unaffected.

## A preliminary conclusion

Our purpose in this chapter has been to develop the concept of
cognitive praxis through exemplification. We have focused on the
dimensions of cognitive praxis, rather than the individual articulators of that praxis, the movement intellectuals. Before turning our
attention to those movement intellectuals, however, it might be
useful to pause and point to what we have learned thus far: what
has the identification of cognitive praxis told us about social processes of knowledge production?

On the one hand, we have shown the active role that social
movements play in translating scientific ideas into social and political beliefs. In the nineteenth century, as well as in the recent past,
social movements have provided an audience for new scientific
paradigms, but even more so, a politicizing dialogue partner for
scientists presenting new ideas about nature and society. New concepts have been popularized by social movements and they have
been given new, more human, meanings and connotations. The

ideas of evolution and of ecology, as well as the very concepts of sociology and economics, have found in social movements a space to develop, to grow, to take on new, more substantial meaning.

Secondly, our approach has pointed to the historical function of social movements as social laboratories. Again in the nineteenth century as well as in the recent past, social movements have experimented with new ways of producing knowledge, new organizational forms and principles. Experimentation in this regard is also a kind of translation process; social movements have transferred activities that have been applied to natural processes to social or societal processes. Cooperative research, alternative technology, participatory policy-making, technology assessment have all grown out of the cognitive praxis of social movements.

Third, social movements have provided societal, or cultural, critiques of dominant techno-economic paradigms, and in their critiques new paradigms have found sources of inspiration. The critique of mechanization, like the contemporary critique of reductionism and mass production, have made it possible for the radical innovators to formulate their radical new ideas. Obviously, we have only scratched the surface of what is a crucially important mechanism of social and economic transformation, but its contours are at least clear: out of critique grows renovation. The process is not perhaps as direct or systematic as might be hoped, but history does not seem to work very systematically. Indeed, our attempt to make social movements visible by identifying the dimensions of their cognitive praxis might make some small contribution to a "systematization" of technological change, but then the policy makers and the technocrats would have to leave their comfortable habitat and enter into the messy world of social movement.

# 4

# Social movements and
# their intellectuals

## What is an intellectual?

Most sociologists of social movements tend to see movement actors
as falling into one or another bipolar category. Although there are
some shades in between, activists usually come in two shades, the
leaders and the led, the organizers and the individual members.
Creating such easy dichotomies has the consequence that the range
of intellectual activities that is performed by activists in social
movements rarely captures the attention of sociologists. Through
our focus on the cognitive dimension this range of activity becomes
not only visible, but indeed central to the very idea of social
movement. We conceive of social movements primarily as processes through which meaning is constituted. In addition to the instrumental and strategic actions which are a necessary part of social
movement praxis, social movements, we contend, are producers of
knowledge. This makes it possible to recognize the range of intellectual practices that are carried out within social movements as
well as the range of contributions of different actors to the making
of social movements.[1]

All activists in social movements are, in some sense, "movement
intellectuals," because through their activism they contribute to the
formation of the movement's collective identity, to making the
movement what it is. All activists do not participate equally in the
cognitive praxis of social movements, however. Some actors are
more visible as organizers, leaders or spokespersons. This visibility,
often helped along by sources outside the movement like the mass
media, is the basis for the usual distinctions between the leaders
and the led. Paraphrasing Gramsci, we can say that while all activists are intellectuals, all activists do not have the function of intellectuals in social movements.[1]

All intellectuals, from our perspective, emerge in particular contexts: no one is born an intellectual. Rather, those both commonly and in more scholarly accounts referred to as intellectuals are formed in the process of social interaction, through the carrying out of intellectual activities in particular social contexts. One such especially significant context is that opened up by a social movement. Antonio Gramsci in his *Prison Notebooks* distinguished between organic intellectuals, formed in the process of the formation of new historical classes, and traditional intellectuals, who carried out their intellectual activities in traditional intellectual institutions like the church and the academy (Gramsci 1971). We would like to "translate" his terms into the more general language of sociology and thus distinguish between *movement intellectuals*, as those who carry out their tasks within a social movement, and *established intellectuals*, who are formed within established social institutional contexts.

It is common among sociologists and historians to assign to "intellectuals" – that is those who are professionally engaged in the production of ideas or the manipulation of symbols – a central role in the creation of meaning and identity that we have characterized as the core of social movement activity. Most especially among Marxists and their anti-Marxist counterparts it is the artists, writers, journalists and, not least, "professional revolutionaries" who take part in social movements who are seen as the articulators of whatever message a social movement may be trying to express. The term intellectual thus has a special place in discussions of social movements. Intellectuals are said to provide a social movement with ideological direction. Indeed, some analysts go so far as to argue that social movements are created by intellectuals to further their own interests as a "new class" (Konrad and Szelenyi 1979; Gouldner 1979). Environmentalism, for Alvin Gouldner, was thus seen as one of the "newer forms of [the] new class's ideology"; Gouldner contended that its "multi-science character provides an ideological framework that can unite various types of technical intelligentsia," and at the same time be "attractive to many humanistic intellectuals" (Gouldner 1979). For Gouldner, as for many other new class theorists, social movements are seen as vehicles for intellectuals to pursue their own interests. The relations between intellectuals and social movements are thus conflated.

The problem with the traditional understanding is that it offers a static view of both intellectuals and social movements. Both are seen as readymade entities set to play their appointed role on the stage of history. Intellectuals are defined by their particular function or role in society, not in terms of their relations to social movements. Intellectuals are those who earn their living with their minds: they are most often conceptualized as a social category of their own. Opinions differ, of course, as to just what that category consists of – and as to whether it is best seen as a unified group or as a collection of different groups. For Lipset and Dobson (1972), as for many other American sociologists, intellectuals are attributed a special function in modern societies as "producers of culture." Marxist-inspired analysts have conceptualized intellectuals as shaped by the "relations of production." As Bourdieu (1984, 1988) and Gouldner (1979) have put it, intellectuals are carriers of "cultural capital," functioning, like other workers, in a capitalist marketplace. Here, as elsewhere, there is usually posited a conflict between those intellectuals who try to uphold some kind of historical mission, or normative ethos, and those intellectuals who seek to serve the highest bidder. What Gouldner has called the "culture of critical discourse" and what others have referred to as intellectual detachment is usually contrasted to a kind of entrepreneurial ideal (Gouldner 1985; Ross 1989). The intellectual as social critic is pitted against the intellectual as professional expert as two competing paradigms of intellectual activity. In most accounts, the expert is seen as the victor, and the critical, or "public intellectual" (Jacoby 1987) is seen to have largely disappeared from the scene.

For sociologists of science, intellectuals are usually seen as scientific practitioners, pursuing a scientific "role" (Ben-David 1971) in modern society; and this role of institutionalized professional scientist is assumed to be the paradigmatic intellectual role in modern societies. For all those who study intellectuals, however, from whichever vantage point they choose, the particular kinds of relations that develop in the context of social movements are not considered as formative influences on intellectual life.

For most sociologists, the intellectuals who take part in social movements do so from their position as intellectuals, not as activists among equals. They are playing their intellectual role, serving their functional time merely in a different "movement" organization. As such, what is special to the interaction between movements and intellectuals, more particularly the new intellectual activities which are created by social movements, is completely lost from sight. Individual intellectuals who take part in movements are transformed into leaders, whether they actually are leaders or not, and they are expected to play the role of ideologist or strategic planner of movement activities. Looked at collectively as a social stratum, intellectuals or the intelligentsia are thus given the mission of providing social movements with leadership and direction.

This "class analysis" of intellectuals and their place in social movements is derived from the Marxian tradition, and in particular the period of social democratic party building in the late nineteenth and early twentieth centuries, when many intellectuals took part in working-class movements. For Karl Kautsky in Germany and then for Lenin in Russia, the intellectual was seen as essential for the development of revolutionary consciousness. "The vehicle of science is not the proletariat," Kautsky wrote in a passage which Lenin later quoted with approval, "but the bourgeois intelligentsia: it was in the minds of individual members of this stratum that modern socialism originated, and it was they who communicated it to the more intellectually developed proletarians who, in their turn, introduce it into the proletarian class struggle where conditions allow that to be done. Thus, socialist consciousness is something introduced into the proletariat class struggle from without and not something that arose within it spontaneously" (Lenin 1977: 40).

As Lenin put it, it was a "profound mistake" to "imagine that the labour movement pure and simple can elaborate, and will elaborate, an independent ideology for itself" (p. 39). The intellectual, in Leninist terms, represents the "interests" of a class that cannot represent itself, formulating the universal interests of mankind in socialist ideology, while the workers themselves can only articulate a "working class consciousness." For Leninists – and it can be argued that all analysts of intellectuals are in some sense Leninists – intellectuals represent a higher set of values that activists or workers or the masses cannot themselves formulate. Thus revolutions, indeed all change in society, are the work of intellectual vanguards who formulate the projects that the masses then realize.

## The formation of movement intellectuals

Our approach represents an attempt to avoid the political and scientific assumptions that underlie such views. We prefer to speak of movement intellectuals and to focus on the formative processes of a social movement, placing both intellectuals and movements in their contexts, rather than defining either as a ready-formed entity and then describing their interaction. Thus we use the term movement intellectual to refer to those individuals who through their activities articulate the knowledge interests and cognitive identity of social movements. They are movement intellectuals because they create their individual role at the same time as they create the movement, as new individual identities and a new collective identity take form in the same interactive process.

By movement intellectuals we do not in the first instance mean those established individuals who perform their intellectual functions in the context of a social movement, or who represent some kind of transcendental intellectual "role" within the space created by social movements. Rather, by identifying intellectual roles and activities within different social movements, and by focusing on the formative processes of movements themselves, we want to develop a different conception of intellectuals altogether. By conceiving of intellectual activity as process rather than product, we also want to uncover the significance of social movements in the societal formation of intellectual activity.

While we agree about the importance of established intellectuals in the formation of many social movements, it is equally important to see that the role and character of intellectuals and of their activities changes as a social movement grows into a more self-conscious social actor. Many, if not all, social movements initially emerge on the basis of some kind of intellectual activity, usually, but not always, carried out by "established" intellectuals. Intellectuals as social critics often play a crucial role in articulating the concerns of emergent forms of protest, putting them into broader frameworks, giving specific protest actions a deeper meaning or significance.

With the coming of new organizations and a more conscious movement identity, however, the relation between movement and intellectual often undergoes a fundamental transformation. Many of the social critics – or established intellectuals – who were active in the early period of awakening choose to remain outside of the actual movement "space" and continue to work in other contexts, while the needs of the new organizations call forth new kinds of intellectuals, often without any formal legitimacy in the established intellectual contexts. These movement intellectuals do not last for ever, however. There is in most movements a tendency toward professionalization that affects the relations between movement organizations and their "organic" intellectuals. As the movement develops, there are almost inevitably tensions between organizations and between individuals in different organizations over these different intellectual roles. Eventually, as the knowledge interests of social movements diffuse into the broader society, many of the new types of professional intellectuals who have been formed within the movement seek legitimacy in more established intellectual contexts: universities, media, industry, etc. As such, they leave the space of the movement to try to establish new professional identities in the larger society. In order to capture these shifts in intellectual roles, it is necessary to see social movements as processes that, as it were, "form" for a time the intellectuals they need.

A necessary condition for the formation of a social movement is the generation of movement intellectuals. However, the line of demarcation between the two categories of established and movement intellectuals is very fluid. As we will show in our examples, established forms and fields of intellectual activity, and of course the activities of established intellectuals, are reinterpreted and expanded through contact with social movements, and, in turn, many movement intellectuals go on to pursue established intellectual traditions and professional careers as movements or their own interests in them wane. With only a little tongue-in-cheek we can say that we reverse the direction given in Leninist models; for us it is movements, as cognitive praxis, that lead and direct intellectuals rather than intellectuals that lead and direct movements.

## Contexts of communication

The societal mode of communication represents an extremely significant conditioning context for both movement intellectuals and established intellectuals. The ideas that intellectuals express must be communicated and the means of this communication are socially determined and change over time. This obviously has a major effect on the way intellectual activity is carried out – both within and outside social movements. Since the early twentieth century, there has been an increasing professionalization of intellectual activity in modern societies, and there has also been an increasing "technification" of the means of communication (Gouldner 1976). The spoken and printed word have become ever more mediated through technologies of "mass communication" and "mass media." And, as a result, the knowledge interests of social movements have grown ever more dependent on the social and technical forms in which these mediated images are communicated. The reception of these mediated images depends at least as much on the frameworks of meaning constituted by the media as on those of the receiver (Gitlin 1980). And this, in turn, has the effect of making the use of professionals and professional skills more acute, something which has greatly affected the formation and even the very occurrence of social movements.

Social movements cannot (yet) employ their own television stations (religious "movements" are the exception) in the way that the older social movements of the nineteenth century owned their own printing companies and movements today in some European countries own their own daily newspapers. It is in part because of their dependence on the "neutral" mass media that the new movements make use of noncommitted professionals more than did older social movements, since the media, the message, and the public have changed. Now movements employ their own professionals, and this is both a source of tension and a contributing factor to the tendency among sociologists to mistake social movements for organizations.

For us, when a movement begins to employ professionals, it marks a shift in the particular movement's identity. It also signifies a shift in relation between that movement and the established political culture: it marks a step in the direction of "incorporation" of the movement, its transformation into an institution. At a more structural level, however, the use of professionals in social movements reflects a shift in intellectual life itself, a shift from the classical amateur, cultivating intellectual pursuits as an avocation or calling, to the modern professional, for whom intellectual work is a vocation, a source of "class, status and power" to use the famous phrase associated with Max Weber. For us, the shift also reflects a transformation in the formative context of movements and intellectuals. The classical amateur was most often a partisan, formulating ideologies or articulating beliefs for the opposing sides in the social movements of the nineteenth century. The professional, on the other hand, is most often a specialist, making use of particular skills and talents in the space created by social movements. While this shift has been noted by many theorists of social movements, what is often ignored is the ways in which those very professional skills are formed by the needs and interests – what we call the cognitive praxis – of social movements. It is in this way, by carving out spaces for new intellectual "types" or roles to develop, that social movements help re-form intellectual life itself. At the same time, social movements also create the possibilities for professionals to expand the bounds of their specialized knowledge by applying it in new, politicized contexts, making it possible for at least some professionals to become movement intellectuals.

In the formative phases of a movement what might be called the classical intellectual role of articulating needs and interests, the role of ideologue and facilitator is of great importance. This classical role has been greatly modified in late modern societies where the wonders of electronics have made communication with a large and faceless "mass" into something different than it was in the social movements of the past. As the commercial and public media discover a movement, new roles and new actors come to the fore. One such new actor is the movement communicator, those particular movement intellectuals who represent the movement to and before the public through the mass media. In the following chapter, we will describe the importance of Martin Luther King's rhetorical abilities and the significance of television for the changing course and image of the American civil rights movement. Persons like Jerry Rubin and Abby Hoffman, creators of the Yippies, a part of the American countercultural movement in the late 1960s, offer another, quite different, example of movement communicators. They created the semblance of a movement with the help of carefully constructed and executed "media events."

In its early phases a budding social movement must constitute itself through more or less traditional means of mobilization, by creating its own organizations and its own networks in order to create a sense of collectivity and to insure its continuity over time and place (Gamson 1975). Here the articulating role of the classical movement intellectual and the information facilitating role of its modern variant are central. In mobilizing a sense of collective will, as well as in articulating felt needs, the classical movement intellectual thematizes in speeches, tracts, articles, and books the rudiments of a new collective identity. Central to this process of self-formation is the constitution of an Other against which the budding movement will interact (Touraine 1981). Thus, one theme facilitating the constitution of a movement's collective identity is the Other against which protest is directed and against whom it will act.

This Other is not merely an intellectual construction, but is almost always a real social actor, an authority, the government, an institution, the state, or a conglomerate of individuals, the "technocrats," with whom the movement must strategically interact. In the process of interaction, other types of movement intellectuals come into play: those who act as intermediaries between the movement and its Other, translating aspects of the movement's newly articulated worldview into programs from which specific demands can be turned into negotiable items in the arenas of the established political culture. Movement spokespeople and experts thus filter out aspects of a rather diffuse worldview, which as a source of collective identity has served as a framework for mobilizing supporters, into clearly defined items for political negotiation in the institutional frameworks of the established political culture. This is not an unproblematic process, as it involves much internal debate and conflict. Never a matter of free choice, the issues and the arenas of confrontation are often forced upon movements by their opponents, the situation, or by the political culture in which they emerge. This can also lead to "diplomatic" negotiators coming to the fore as significant movement intellectuals. Much as the media can impose one kind of intellectual type on movements, so can the peculiarities of the political culture.

Let us now illustrate these perhaps overly abstract points about movement intellectuals through examples taken from actual social movements.

## Movement intellectuals in the environmental movement

In our studies of environmentalism, we have identified a range of movement intellectuals who have been formed in the social space created by this movement (Jamison et al., 1990). The environmental movement emerged in large measure from the activity of established intellectuals, thus seemingly giving support to traditional accounts of the role of intellectuals in social movements. It was out of the writings of ecologists and conservationists and perhaps especially popular science writers that the cognitive identity of environmental activism first came to be articulated. These were, for the most part, persons who were already socially legitimated intellectuals, either through their academic position (Barry Commoner, Paul Ehrlich, René Dubos, George Borgström) or through their popular writings (Rachel Carson, Lewis Mumford, Vance Packard).

Rachel Carson's *Silent Spring* (1962) was one of the central intellectual sparks which ignited the movement. It was probably no accident that it was a woman with both academic credentials and literary skills who most dramatically awakened the general public, in the United States and elsewhere, to the environmental "crisis." Rachel Carson's previous books, especially *The Sea Around Us*, had won for her a reputation as a serious popularizer of natural science. They also ensured her access to the popular media, so that her *Silent Spring* could first appear in the prestigious weekly magazine *New Yorker* in 1960 and then on the mass paperback market almost immediately following its booklength publication in 1962.

The other main writings of the 1960s which articulated the knowledge interests of the environmental movement were also the work of relatively established intellectuals. Having already achieved legitimation in the eyes of their colleagues or peers, they could critically challenge dominant conceptions of nature and societal practices that affected the natural environment, thus opening up a space within which the "environment" could be re-cognized as an area for social political debate. Drawing on the findings of established scientists, as well as on the new conceptualizations of systems ecology, these writers could begin to formulate an alternative ecological worldview, as well as an alternative technological paradigm, the biological "other road" that Carson outlined in her critique of chemical pesticides. In the course of the 1960s, these early premonitions would grow ever more explicit as environmental protest took on more coherent form. By 1972, when Barry Commoner's *The Closing Circle* was published (again after serialization in *New Yorker*), a range of new organizations had been created on the basis of numerous protest actions and "earth day" manifestations. By then, a movement was forming, ready to receive Commoner's explicit "laws of ecology." What had been only vaguely articulated as a critique of the "central dogma" of biology in Commoner's first book, *Science and Survival* (1966) was now a programmatic formulation of a movement identity (Commoner 1966, 1972).

Established intellectuals were thus crucial in laying the groundwork for the formation of the environmental movement, but it would be a mistake to claim that they created the movement. The knowledge interests of modern environmentalism were constituted only when a new public space had been carved out, when a new form of cognitive praxis emerged under the influence of the student revolts of the late 1960s. The written and spoken works of established intellectuals were not enough in and of themselves; the

knowledge interests of the environmental movement required for
their specification "external" stimulation as well (Jamison et al.
1990). The essential point is that established intellectuals together
with new movement activists carved out a public space, an "opportunity structure" as the current jargon would have it, for the articulation of new environmental knowledge interests.

In order to contribute to the making of a social movement it
was necessary for the established intellectuals to recontextualize
their intellectual activity (Mitchell 1979). The critical scientists and
science writers who wrote about environmental problems in the
1960s operated within established intellectual contexts, but those
who helped to "make" the movement could not continue to carry
out their activity as they had traditionally done. For one thing, they
changed the intended audience for their intellectual production,
writing and speaking no longer primarily for their colleagues and
students but for a "general public." And with the change of audience came also a change of media, from scientific journals and
academic lectures to popular books and articles and public meetings.

Even more importantly, the movement builders took part in a
process of recombination: they combined their expertise with that
of others in creating a movement space of new environmental
organizations, protests, magazines, etc. And as that movement
space broadened, in the development of new environmentalist
organizations through the 1970s, nonestablished intellectuals, often
students, took over from the established intellectuals in the further
articulation and specification of environmentalist knowledge interests or movement identity. In a sense, a line was drawn which
many established intellectuals were not able or willing to cross. A
new type of movement intellectual began to translate the concerns
of these critical scientists into the core identity of what was becoming a social movement. These particular movement intellectuals
helped define the relations to other movements and social actors,
facilitating the flow of knowledge from one movement to another
and translating or interpreting the message of the movement into
other discourses.[2]

In the case of environmentalism, a particular type of movement
intellectual was important already at these early stages of movement formation: the counterexpert, challenging the decisions and
standards of the governmental environmental experts on behalf of
an emerging "public interest." In some countries, these counterex-

perts were primarily biologists or biology students, in others they were lawyers or law students, and in still others, where occupational health formed part of the new environmentalist agenda, medical doctors and students took on the mantle of the counterexpert. Most, if not all, of these movement intellectuals had received education or professional training during the late 1960s, and were thus influenced in the choice of occupation and intellectual strategy by the concerns of the student movement. In Sweden, Denmark, and the Netherlands, the countries that formed the basis of our own comparative research, this formative influence was particularly striking (Jamison et al., 1990). In other countries, such as Great Britain and the United States, counterexperts were formed to a somewhat larger extent within already established conservation societies, and were formed as part of "internal" revolts and breakaways against a conservation establishment (Hays 1987; Lowe and Goyder 1983).

Environmentalism emerged as a movement while most national states were developing new agencies and legislation to deal with the environmental problems that had been brought to public consciousness. In formulating their counterarguments to the governmental standards and procedures, these movement intellectuals served to specify the Other against which the movement developed its own identity. The counterexperts opposed not merely the state and its environmental bureaucracies, but also the elitist conceptualization of knowledge epitomized by state experts (and established conservation societies). The counterexpert as movement intellectual symbolized a democratic ideal, a sharing of knowledge, thus embodying the organizational dimension of the emergent movement's knowledge interests (Cotgrove 1982).

As the movement developed in the course of the 1970s, other types of intellectual activity performed by movement intellectuals took form within the environmental movement. There are those who can be referred to as grassroots engineers, who directed a kind of sociotechnical learning process among environmental activists, those people who taught short courses in renewable energy, alternative agriculture, recycling, etc. (Boyle and Harper 1976). In a country like Denmark, where technological development has historically been decentralized, these grassroots engineers became especially significant in articulating the identity of the environmental movement. A manual written by two student activists, on solar and wind energy, became a minor bestseller in movement circles, and a national network of local "energy offices" was created to stimulate 'grassroots' engineering. For several years in the late 1970s, the world's largest windmill stood at the small town of Tvind in western Denmark, the result of an alternative engineering praxis in a community of alterntive schools, a movement space carved out by enterprising student activists (Jamison 1978).

Still another type of environmental movement intellectual were the public educators who popularized the message of the movement in the pamphlets and magazines and even posters that became the main vehicles of information dissemination. Some of these public educators specialized in public speaking, others in writing, still others in media, debating with the opposition, the established energy officials, and environmental authorities.

Often such movement intellectuals have not assumed any formal leadership role in the movement, but were, and in many cases still are, activists among others. Indeed, in the case of contemporary social movements at least, most activists are movement intellectuals in one form or another and at one time or another. That is part of the very idea of a social movement: by spontaneously responding to new social problems, indeed often formulating those problems for society, social movements create spaces for new exploratory intellectual activities to crystallize.[3]

As the environmental movement grew to prominence, however, particularly in the struggles against nuclear energy, many of these movement intellectuals tended to become ever more professional, at the same time as new types of professional consultants, publicists, and debaters entered the scene to "take over" from the movement organizations. This tendency towards professionalization has perhaps been especially strong in environmentalist movements where science and technology play such a central role. Challenging the claims of government and private corporations has often entailed engaging in scientific debates about the feasibility and desirability of particular techniques or policies. The counterknowledge and legal help necessary to such argumentation requires that movement organizations either seek voluntary help from sympathetic specialists or hire short-term consultants. Trade unions and the labor movement face different but related problems in their need to hire professionals to help with complicated collective bargaining agreements, internal education, and political lobbying. The need for professionals also concerns the administration of movement organizations, which in today's highly organized societies is ever more intensified.

A related reason for professionalization of intellectual activities in the environmental movement was simply the need to coordinate and communicate effectively among ever growing numbers of local groups and individual members. If it is to last and expand, a social movement must create an effective communication network between its various groups and organizations, as well as mediate the relationship between the individual and the collective, including the movement and the public. In this process, local organizational structures are at least as important as national leadership, and non-credentialed movement intellectuals as important as their credentialed counterparts. A highly organized complex society, however, encourages formally organized and structured movements of opposition. This creates the possibility of tensions not only between local and national levels of movement organization, but also between types of movement intellectuals.

The American environmental movement offers an example of such a tension and of a radical fragmentation between locally based, nonprofessional grassroots organizations and highly professionalized national organizations. The structure of American politics and political traditions of locallybased participatory democracy contributed to this fragmentation. With the federal government located in Washington, DC, structured through a two-party system of representative democracy which is open to the lobbying efforts of special interest groups, and local and state governments open to pressure from citizen action groups, American social movements face the dilemma of trying to be both formal, professional lobbying organizations and single-issue grassroots organizations. As far as environmentalism is concerned this led to a "movement" that has existed almost from its inception as two deeply divided fragments: professionally run and hierarchically organized pressure groups like Sierra Club and National Wildlife Federation on the one hand; and local, often quite temporary, action groups and alliances on the other (O'Brien 1983).

In the 1980s, the environmental movement all but split apart in most countries, and with it came the new phenomenon of the totally professionalized environmental organization in the guise of Greenpeace International, one of the largest and most effective environmental organizations (Eyerman and Jamison 1989). Greenpeace is centrally steered and hierarchically organized, run by administrative professionals who hire technical and specialist help on a short-term basis and who radically restrict supporters to the role of temporary office help and anonymous financial donor. Its relations to its public and its opponents is also highly mediated and professional. Campaigns are carefully planned and run with militarylike efficiency to achieve the most effect and visibility in the mass media. The object of such campaigns, however, is mostly publicity that is, fundraising efforts for the real work, which is pressure on governments and private corporations. Direct mailing follows such campaigns and potential support is tapped. There is thus little direct contact between activists and the public or their opponents. This is certainly a long remove from the leaflet and the newspaper which has served as a means of direct contact or communication between the activist and the public. The public is also tapped through opinion polls and surveys and the sale of articles like T-shirts and pins. Such activity not only creates a different type of relation to public and opponent alike but a different kind of intellectual: the highly effective manager and highly organized professional activist.

Along with Greenpeace have come the Green parties, with their parliamentary professionalization of environmental politics, and the professionalization of environmental science and technology as well. Throughout the world, a new range of environmentalist professions are entering the established contexts of intellectual life. Almost all universities have by now established environmental studies departments, staffed with environmental engineers and scientists. Industrial firms have seen a new market in the greening of society, and have also established environmental departments with new fangled experts. Law schools train environmental lawyers, and schools of journalism train environmental writers. There are even artists and writers and other more traditional intellectual types who have specialized themselves to environmentalist themes. As the movement has all but ceased to exist as a relatively autonomous public space, its movement intellectuals have grown into new kinds of established intellectuals.

## Classical partisan intellectuals

Precursors to the movement intellectual types which we have found in the environmental movements can be found in the labor movement. Indeed, it was within those movements that the very idea of the public intellectual emerged as a social concept. Previously, intellectual activity was not seen as characteristic of a particular social group or group of actors, it was something done within other vocations and institutional roles. Clergymen and later university professors can of course be seen as intellectuals, but their standing in society was not derived from their intellectual activity as such so much as from their institutional affiliation. Clergymen served God and professors trained clergymen and later civil servants and doctors, but they were not intellectuals in anything like a modern sociological sense. Intellectuals could not exist as a self-conscious group, that is, as a social actor, until "society" itself had been conceptualized; and that, we claim, was largely the work of the social movements of the nineteenth century. As sociology itself was the product of the labor movement and the transition to modernity, so was the intellectual.[4] From Marx and Engels and their *Communist Manifesto* of 1848, which sought to explain to "the proletariat" just what their historical role was, to the Kautskys and Bebels of the late nineteenth century formulating the programs of the social democratic parties, the public intellectual was first and foremost the self-appointed formulator of political ideology.

It was not only ideas that gave to the new intellectuals a cohesive sense of mission, but also new means of communication. New mass media like the daily newspaper, coupled with the extension of literacy, made it possible to reach wider segments of the population with an ideological message. In the revolution of 1848, Karl Marx spent much of his time and talent in starting and editing the *Neue Rheinische Zeitung* (later he worked as a reporter for the New York *Tribune*), and a little more than 50 years later, Lenin ended his now famous phamplet *What Is to be Done?* with a call to organize not a new party but a new newspaper. "Launching a newspaper," writes Alvin Gouldner, "is something that workers and artisans are less likely than intellectuals to define as a vital political act" (Gouldner 1985: 121). Yet, for the emerging working class, gaining self-awareness through the labor movement, this use of the new mass media proved vital, even where many activists remained suspicious of those partisan "bourgeois" intellectuals who worked on them. As Lenin recognized, newspapers were useful not only as means for spreading ideas but also for organizing collective identity and coordinating action. Newspapers and, in the absence of what Antonio Gramsci was later to call an "organic" working intelligentsia, partisan intellectuals were vital to the very formation of the movement and through it of the class itself.

This importance was not confined to socialist intellectuals and to the working-class movements; conservatism and liberalism had their own "public," their own partisan spokesmen, and their news-papers, But it was largely through the social democratic – and later communist – party formation that the role of partisan intellectual took on a paradigmatic form. The formulation and dissemination of ideas, however, meant taking on many different roles: publicist, public educator, teacher, and perhaps most importantly, adver-saries of the experts of the established political order that the movements were challenging. With substantial variations, these roles have nonetheless recurred in various guises from movement to movement, as the classical model of the partisan intellectual of the nineteenth century has been reinterpreted and thus reinvented in the contexts of subsequent social movements.

In the early part of the twentieth century, in conjunction with the collapse of the established political order at the end of the First World War and the radicalization of working class movements in Hungary and Germany, this model was given new content. In a series of newspaper and journal articles, the Hungarian writer and critic Georg Lukács called upon established intellectuals to join these movements not as leaders, but rather as seekers of knowledge and truth. For Lukács, active participation in social movements, that is, direct engagement in politics, was a precondition for truly understanding the social world. Without such partisan engagement alongside the working class, the "bourgeois" intellectual would remain caught in the fragmented world of class-based false con-sciousness (Lukacs 1972). He wrote:

> "Intellectual leadership" can only be one thing: the process of mak-ing social development consicous ... the "knowledge" ... that the "laws" governing social development, their complete independence of human consciousness, their similarity with the play of the blind forces of nature, are a mere appearance which can serve only until those blind forces have been awakened to consciousness by this knowledge.... But this mission [of leadership] cannot be the pri-vilege of any "intellectual class" or the product of any "supra-class" thinking ... only through the class consciousness of the proletarians is it possible to achieve the knowledge to intellectual leadership. (pp. 17–18)

Thus for Lukács, the participation of established intellectuals in social movements was a precondition for their own intellectual development; only through such participation could they gain the "true" knowledge they sought. Lukács reversed the predominant

Russian Bolshevik and German social democratic ideas concerning the role of the established intellectual in working-class movements. From this point of view, the established intellectual had no higher moral or cognitive standing *vis à vis* the working class, no social responsibilty in that sense. Rather he or she had an "intellectual" responsibility to participate, a responsibility to knowledge and truth, which were the promised outcome of activism. Knowledge of the social world was thus linked to a common struggle for political emancipation, something which removed its possession from any particular individual or social group. Political activism was for Lukács the quintessence of intellectual activity: it was the path along which enlightenment and emancipation were reunited.[5] Intellectuals were those who participated: the mantle was won and worn in context, through activism, not before.

Taken seriously, this point of view removed the established intellectual from his/her institutionally legitimated pedestal; all activists were, in theory, made common partners in the struggle for enlightenment through political engagement. There might be an internal division of labor in that struggle, a division based on function, but no hierarchy based upon class or culturally based claims to superior knowledge was possible.

This position was given a similar, though less radical, formulation by another partisan intellectual of the same period, Antonio Gramsci. Gramsci, who as a student worked as a journalist for socialist newspapers in Turin and later as an editor and writer on other party journals, was jailed for his political activities by Mussolini and died in prison in 1937. In what were later published as his *Prison Notebooks* (1971) he formulated his thoughts on the role of the partisan intellectual. Gramsci separated the intellectual activity as profession from critical thinking as such. Organized into professions in hierarchically ordered class society, cognitive activity may be the province of a particular social class or stratum thereof, but as a human capacity, critical thinking was open to all. One aim of the working-class movement, Gramsci argued, was just that of overcoming this division, making its emancipatory aims cognitive and cultural as well as political in the narrow sense. Thus the participation of "traditional" (established) intellectuals as partisan activists in the working-class movement aimed at eliminating a social hierarchy based on knowledge. Ideally this aim should be reflected in the very organization of the movement itself, in its nonhierarchical and antibureaucratic factory councils and its cultural organizations.

As working-class movements established themselves, more

formalized organizationally situated "intellectual" roles were instituted. It became possible to support oneself as a movement intellectual. Rosa Luxemburg, one of the leading public figures of the Polish and German left in the early part of the century, provides a good example of the practice of being a partisan intellectual. Like Gramsci, Luxemburg began her activism as a student working on a movement newspaper. She later was cofounder, editor-in-chief and main contributor to *The Workers' Cause*, a newspaper associated with the Polish social democratic party. After fleeing to Germany, she wrote articles for German social democratic newspapers, in whose pages she carried on a masterful polemic against both reformist leaders of the party like Eduard Bernstein and Lenin's ideas concerning the role of organization and knowledge in the movement (Ettinger 1987: 85). These articles caught the attention of party officials and she was offered the editorship of a local party newspaper. In addition to her journalism, Luxemburg eventually held the chair in political economy at the German social democratic party school, founded in 1906 to provide an alternative education for party and trade union activists. Her position paid well – 3,000 marks a semester. It required her to give two-hour lectures four times a week on political economy, Marxist theory, and the history of trade unions (Ettinger 1987: 181–2). These lectures eventually resulted in her magnum opus *The Accumulation of Capital*. Ideally, such schools were to have a transitionary function, providing a space in which the skills possessed by established intellectuals could be reinterpreted and transmitted to the working class. In addition to providing a means of support for partisan intellectuals, then, the aim of such party schools was to overcome just that knowledge gap that Gramsci pointed out, for the movement to produce its own "organic" intellectuals.

Learning and teaching are quintessential intellectual activities and, as we have just discussed, those established intellectuals who participated in social movements in the nineteenth and early part of the twentieth centuries did so in the role of teacher. That is, they gave their normal occupation new content with their social movement participation: teaching the uneducated massses about the "real" nature of their society and social position. Thus the connection between social movements as collective public action and intellectuals as public actors *par excellence* seems almost natural.

Intellectual activity is also public activity in another sense; it involves public performance, presentation, argumentation, dialogue: the communicative interaction between speaker and listener. However, as noted, and as is present in nearly all situations and interactions between teacher and taught, there is often a built-in inequality, not to say manipulation, in this relation. The cognitive practice of teaching, the relation between teacher and taught, as well as the media involved in that public activity, have all substantially changed from the nineteenth century to the present, thus substantially affecting the relation between intellectual and social movements.

### From intellectual-in-movement to movement intellectual

The classical nineteenth-century partisan intellectual was an intellectual-in-movement, part of an elite grounded in high culture, usually with a humanist education, often using his or her "higher standpoint" to claim insight into the "laws of history and society," giving to themselves the task of leading "blind" social forces. Their movement intellectual practice consisted largely in the attempt, through their spoken and written texts, as well as through organizational infighting, to influence the understanding and the activities of other movement actors. Marx and Engels are the classical example. The partisan intellectual as ideologist and teacher often played the role of gatekeeper, deciding what was relevant for discussion and who was competent to participate. This function developed later on within social movement organizations and communication networks, when the role of ideologist was institutionalized to include editing a newspaper or running a meeting.

There are substantial differences between the activities performed by the classical partisan intellectual of the nineteenth century and the movement intellectuals of the late twentieth. Where many partisan intellectuals often served as leaders, even rulers, of the parties and organizations that they spoke for, contemporary movement intellectuals are usually more limited and specialized in their role. The partisan intellectual of the nineteenth century often lives on, however, as a role model, particularly among "leaders" of organizations and parties, and perhaps even more as an inspirational figure of almost mythological proportions. For many interpreters of social movements, this idea of the intellectual as prophetic hero colors their accounts and thereby diverts attention from the actual intellectual activity that movement intellectuals carry out.

## From old to new movements

What has changed in the historical space between the old social movements of the nineteenth and early twentieth centuries and the new social movements discussed previously is the structure and the process of constituting the public and its "interests." Crucial here is the development of mass media, mass culture, and mass education. About the first, the mass media, Todd Gitlin (1980) has written:

> The New Left of the 1960s, facing nightly television news, wire service reports, and a journalistic ideology of "objectivity", inhabited a cultural world vastly different from that of the Populist small farmers' movement [in America] of the 1890s, with its fifteen hundred autonomous weekly newspapers, or that of the worker-based Socialist Party of the early 1900s, with its own newspapers circulating in the millions. (p. 2)

Gitlin goes on to say that the United States in the 1960s "was the first society in the history of the world with more college students than farmers." Such changes cannot but greatly affect the cognitive praxis of social movements and the form and content of the activities of movement intellectuals. While some of the activities and functions performed by the classical partisan intellectual still form a part of the social movement repertoire, contemporary social movements, measured in terms of the years of formal education of activists, are largely movements of intellectuals. The gap between the educated leaders and the "masses" has been significantly diminished, and the claim to privileged insight on the basis of a higher cultural understanding is, justifiably, regarded with skepticism if not totally discredited as "ideology" (Gouldner 1979; Bell 1962). As opposed to the classical intellectual-in-movement, today's movement intellectual moves in a world of popular culture and mass education. Still, the educating function and the ideological consciousness of the movement intellectual continues to exist, both internally in terms of the politicizing effects on activists and supporters and in terms of addressing and attempting to influence the general public. However, along with the levelling effect of formal education, the means of communicating with and addressing the public have radically altered with the advent of electronic mass communication, thus also affecting the intellectual praxis of social movements and of movement intellectuals.[6]

One central task of the movement intellectual is that of providing a larger framework of meaning in which individual and collective actions can be understood. In classical terms this role was connected to the production and dissemination of ideology. While this role is still present to a degree in contemporary social movements, the praxis of movement intellectuals is today at once more generally available and more mediated. The commercialization of cultural experience, which undermined the idea of "high culture," has removed the platform from which "intellectuals" could claim privileged insight. But at the same time new barriers have been built: the mass media and in particular its electronic variant have distanced the leaders from the led.

The American student movement was in many ways the precursor and model for student movements around the world. It began in small-scale local conflicts concerning particular issues, which also expressed or would come to express general themes: the meaning and purpose of education, the role of the university in society, and the relations of subordinates to authority. While it is difficult to set an exact date and place to its origins, the Free Speech Movement at the University of California at Berkeley in 1964 is both a convenient and useful starting point.

These were the first rumblings of a general student unrest in American society. But deeper cognitive as well as organizational roots can be traced back to 1962 when a small group of university students met in Port Huron, Michigan, and formed the Students for a Democratic Society (SDS). Under the auspices of a left of centre group called the League for Industrial Democracy, a group of students and older political activists met to hammer out a program for the mounting of a national student movement. What emerged from this meeting was a loosely formulated program which later became known as the Port Huron Statement, a document which attempted to formulate the feelings of a new generation of college students raised in the quietness of suburban living and dissatisfied with its smug privilege (Sale 1974; Miller 1987; Gitlin 1987). Written in the form of a political tract, it was primarily the work of one person, Tom Hayden, the young editor of the college newspaper at the University of Michigan in nearby Ann Arbor. Acting more as a secretary and a facilitator and coordinator of discussion rather than ideologue, Hayden presented in systematized form the results of these meetings in the form of a document. In fact, ideology played if anything only a negative role in the birthpangs of the

American student movement, functioning in its liberal or Marxist variants as something to be avoided.

It was perhaps no accident that Hayden was at the time in the process of writing a master's thesis on C. Wright Mills, who in many respects had come to epitomize the alternative intellectual role that the SDS students were seeking (Miller 1987). Mills was one of the few established academics in the 1950s to continue to write critically about American society and American intellectuals. Just before he died in 1961, he had written an article in a new student journal, calling for a "new left," where he wrote that "the end-of-ideology is in reality the ideology of an ending: the ending of political reflection itself as a public fact. It is a weary know-it-all justification – by tone of voice rather than explicit argument – of the cultural and political default of the NATO intellectuals" (Mills 1963: 249).

Mills was one of the inspirational sources for the new movement intellectual identity that was being formed in SDS. What the SDS founders articulated in the Port Huron statement was a reservoir of standpoints and interests that would come to be drawn upon both by students and other social groups as the American student movement took form. Central to that movement was a critique of the intellectual as specialized expert and of the reduction of intellectual activity to intellectual labor due to the change in the structure and function of the university.[7] Connected to this was an activist conception of intellectual activity, a sense that knowledge must be put to good and better use.[8]

At least as important as the content was the process through which the document was produced. In fact, it can be argued that the process, what was later given the name "participatory democracy," constitutes the real contribution of the American student movement to the new politics of the last decades (Miller 1987). As the phrase indicates, participatory democracy meant that all participants were (potentially) equal and capable not only of understanding the significance of but also of making a social movement. Thus the gap between the leaders and the led was also attacked in the process. Both the idea and the practice of participatory democracy criticized the classical role of the intellectual in regard to the "old" labor movement, favoring the movement intellectual as facilitator, interpreter, and synthesizer, rather than ideological leader.

The activity of the movement intellectual mixes intellectual and political activism in a particular way and in a particular context.

The context is that of a social movement, where a great deal of the intellectual activity is centered arround the formation of a collective identity (Melucci 1989).[9] As noted, one central aspect of this process is the construction of the Other, the opposition, against which the movement is protesting and struggling. The Other, however, is not merely the symbolic construction of movement intellectual activity, it also refers to real social actors in real arenas of action, all of which are historically and culturally conditioned and which must be dealt with strategically as well as communicatively. Social movements are after all political phenomena, operating in established political cultural contexts, a point stressed by resource mobilization theorists and often forgotten by those, like Melucci (1989) and Habermas (1987b). who stress the symbolic nature of social movements. Describing how this strategic activity interlaces with the communicative processes of constituting and maintaining collective identity is essential to explaining why particular social movements develop in the ways that they do and what movement intellectuals do in the process.

We can illustrate this through an example, one which at the same time reveals another role performed by classical intellectuals in connection with the political strategies of social movements–the way they through their prestige, provide access to the centers of established power. The peace movement is always included as one of the three "new" social movements. In Great Britain, perhaps the core of the peace movement is the CND, the Campaign for Nuclear Disarmament.[10] The CND was formed in 1957 in the context of the cold war, atomic bomb tests and the Suez crisis. With no parliamentary party willing to speak out in favor of unilateral nuclear disarmament and the end to nuclear testing, local groups of extra-parliamentary opposition began to form. When it became clear that even the left wing of the Labour party would not support nuclear disarmament, a group of well-known intellectuals, including Bertrand Russell and Julian Huxley, formed the CND with Russell as its president (Byrne 1988). Although the CND was extraparliamentary in its formation, the political inclination of the founding members was decidedly toward influencing the established political institutions through the personal prestige and social contacts of the founding members, that is, through being an elite pressure group, writing critical articles in established liberal journals and putting pressure on their social peers in positions of power and influence. However, given the great initial public response to the CND, this strategy came almost immediately into question, especially by those who favored the direct action of mass demonstration.

This example is meant to indicate how the cognitive praxis of a movement is strongly conditioned by the particular intellectuals doing the articulating, who are not without allegiances and interests of their own. Established intellectuals are often integrated into structured social networks; in their activity one often finds inbuilt biases toward certain strategies and tactics of protest and change. Given the access that the "British intelligentsia" had to the corridors of power in British society, it was quite natural to attempt to steer CND in the direction of an elite pressure group, rather than a social movement geared to "street politics." That they lost control over the CND and that some of this elite, Russell the most noteworthy, were to engage in street politics reveals the importance of internal conflicts, especially in the early stages, in shaping the form and content of the development of social movements. It also reveals how the processes involved in the formation and maintenance of collective identity are heterogeneous: collective identity is, in many ways, a process of negotiation among the various actors involved (Melucci 1989: 30).

## Conclusion

This chapter aimed at developing the concept of movement intellectual through illustrating the ways in which social movements provide spaces within which intellectual innovation takes place. In the contexts provided by social movements, established identities and practices are transformed as old roles are refitted and reinterpreted in the processes of making a new social movement.

As social and political processes, social movements provide spaces in which the established routines of everyday life are broken, creating opportunities for new social identities and roles to be tried on and tested out. By focusing on the cognitive praxis of social movements, we call attention to the intellectual activity of social movements, to the tension between established practices and innovation. Key actors in this cognitive praxis are those we have identified as movement intellectuals. Movement intellectuals are actors who articulate the collective identity that is fundamental to the making of a social movement. Often it is disenchanted established intellectuals, those with credentials and skills gathered in the institutions of the established society, who play a leading role in this process, especially in the early stages of movement development. However, as opposed to many other theorists concerned with social movements who have pointed this out, we argue that established intellectuals are transformed through their movement activity, even where, as in the last example taken from the CND, they may bring many of their preconceived ideas and social networks, their cultural capital, with them.

Social movements not only create spaces in which established intellectuals and established practices are reinterpreted, they also provide opportunities for new intellectual types to emerge. Through the opportunities created for public expression, in movement newspapers, pamphlets, meetings, etc., individuals without formal training and credentials have the opportunity to learn new skills and to practice them (King 1987). This very opportunity sometimes creates the grounds for internal tensions between established intellectuals and the emerging movement intellectuals, as we will illustrate in more detail in the next chapter.

The particular contexts in which social movements emerge also affect the types of movement intellectuals as well as the form and content of their cognitive praxis. A central part of this praxis was identified as the articulation of the "Other," the opposition, against which the movement will struggle and against which it will itself take shape. This Other is not merely a theoretically constructed object, however, but a real social actor operating through the specific arenas of a political culture. Thus the constitution of the Other involves a selection of levels and contexts in and on which it will be fought: the parliament, the corporation, the public, etc. This selection is not freely made, it is influenced by the opposition and its choices, as well as by the movement intellectuals themselves. The media used in the articulation and the arena of struggle also involve similar selection. The shifting means of communication are important considerations here: they help select not only what skills but also who are core movement intellectuals. We can now turn to our next chapter which, using the American civil rights movement as an example, will attempt to concretize even more these points and processes.

# 5

# A case study: The American civil rights movement

In chapter 1, we argued that conceptions of social movements are conditioned by the political culture in which they are formulated, and, in particular, by the "role" that social movements have played in each political culture. We contended that there were significant differences in how social movements developed in different countries, and that those differences had a strong influence on how social movements were conceptualized by sociologists. The time has now come to take our own claim seriously. In this chapter we will try to put our own concepts in cultural context. We will apply our concepts, in some detail, to the American civil rights movement, indicating how the cognitive praxis of that movement must be related to the "peculiarities" of American political culture. Our case study is meant to show the way our concepts need to be contextualized if they are to be used to analyze particular social movements.

Social movements draw on the intellectual traditions and the types of knowledge that are specific to the societies in which they emerge. But this drawing upon is double-edged in that those traditions condition both the movement and the movement's opposition. The American civil rights movement provides particularly rich material for illustrating this aspect of the process of social movement formation and the mediating role of movement intellectuals. Because of its exceptional character, it also provides a test for the generalizability of our conceptual framework. In this chapter we will examine in some detail the various types of movement intellectuals that emerged in the American civil rights movement. We will also try to characterize the cognitive praxis that the movement articulated.

## The cognitive praxis of the civil rights movement

From our perspective, the cognitive praxis of the civil rights movement developed over time; the movement's project did not emerge
readyformed when the first bus boycotts and sit-ins took place in
the 1950s. In order to understand cognitive praxis as process in
formation, it may be useful to divide the civil rights movement into
four phases, roughly corresponding to the phases that we have used
in our analysis of the contemporary environmental movements. A
similar attempt to periodize the civil rights movement can be found
in McAdam (1982).

The first phase, a period of awakening, can be conveniently
dated to June 1953 with the boycott of the public bus system in
Baton Rouge, Louisiana (Morris 1984). This action came to serve
as a source of inspiration for the more famous events that were
initiated in December 1955, when Rosa Parks refused to give up
her seat to a white man in a city bus in Montgomery, Alabama. The
ensuing bus boycott, which, among other things, brought to public
attention the oratorical talents of a young black minister, Martin
Luther King, Jr, is usually considered the starting point of the civil
rights movement. An important contextual factor was the US Supreme Court decision in 1954, in the case of Brown versus Board of
Education of Topeka, when segregation of public schools was
judged unconstitutional.

The period of awakening lasted until 1960, when a new phase of
movement building began to emerge with the lunch counter sit-ins
in Greensboro, North Carolina, and in other southern cities, which
led to the establishment of the Student Non-violent Coordinating
Committee (SNCC) in April. The creation of SNCC marks a new
phase in the civil rights movement for two main reasons; on the one
hand, the organization brought a new generation of student activists into the developing movement; and on the other, it shifted the
strategic focus of the movement from the defensive orientation of
the bus boycotts to a more offensive direct action. With the emergence of SNCC, the older Congress of Racial Equality (CORE),
established in Chicago in 1947 by black and white college students,
and the recently established Southern Christian Leadership Conference (SCLC) joined together to carve out a new kind of public
space in opposition to the institutionalized activity of the National
Association for the Advancement of Colored People (NAACP).

Where the NAACP stood for legislative reform and judicial strategy, the new movement stood for direct action and mass participation. For a time, the old and new movements could join forces, most impressively in the March on Washington in 1963, but in the late 1960s the movement split apart, as the various organizations went separate ways.

The seeds of dissension were sown in 1964, in the battles at the Democratic National Convention over the seating of a delegation of civil rights activists from Mississippi, a challenge to established practice supported by the new organizations but opposed by NAACP. But the movement split apart most visibly after 1965, when a new phase in the movement can be discerned. The period 1965–69 can be considered the phase of polarization, in which one side of the movement grew increasingly "revolutionary," both inspiring and participating actively in the broader movement against the war in Vietnam, while the other grew increasingly "reformist," entering electoral politics and sketching a program of "black capitalism." In the 1970s, both sides would totally leave a common movement space in a fourth period of incorporation/ marginalization, creating new institutions and organizations to diffuse the ideas that had developed in the movement.

The cognitive praxis of the civil rights movement formed in relation to these phases. In the first period, the twin pillars of legality and spirituality – which would come to be combined in the cognitive praxis of the movement in the 1960s – were still separate. The Supreme Court decision, and many other political contextual factors, led to an affirmation of the legal strategy and the legalistic belief system that was so central to the NAACP. Meanwhile, with King and other black ministers bringing the cultural resources of the southern black church into the fray, the interest in racial equality came to be expressed in religious terms. For us, the dimensions of cognitive praxis remained, in this first phase, implicit. It would be in the early 1960s, in the period of movement building, that the historical project of the movement would be explicitly formulated and articulated as the cognitive identity of a social movement.

At the cosmological level, the movement came to stand for a unique combination of legalism and religiosity. In their actions, movement activists were reaffirming American ideals of equality and democracy, claiming their rights to be included in the mainstream of American life. At the same time, they were embodying archetypical Christian beliefs of redemption and reconciliation, asking their enemies to respect them, appealing to a higher order, and to the moral example of Jesus. The ideal of an integrated society was one around which both whites and blacks could be mobilized. The passionate, even visionary egalitarianism that characterized the civil rights movement can be considered a utopia, in the sense that Mannheim used the term. In SNCC, the utopia was put into practice: "We saw ourselves, black and white together, as a 'band of brothers and sisters' and 'a circle of trust.' The spirit that united us ... was such that we would have died for one another" (Mary King 1987: 297). For Martin Luther King, the utopia was the "dream that one day on the red hills of Georgia the sons of former slaves and the sons of former slaveowners will be able to sit down together at the table of brotherhood" (Martin Luther King, "I Have A Dream," quoted in Gitlin 1987: 146). For activists throughout the movement, the vision of an integrated society where all were equal formed the basis of the shared belief that "deep in my heart, I do believe that we shall overcome someday ..."

The technical dimension of the civil rights movement's cognitive praxis consists of the specific objects of opposition and, even more importantly, the tactics, the techniques of protest, by which those objects were opposed. The moral passion needed to be practiced, and it needed to be able to be practiced by large numbers of people in order to make a social movement. Central to the cognitive praxis of the civil rights movement were the techniques of nonviolent direct action, taught systematically and even professionally by movement intellectuals, many of whom had read of Gandhi's independence struggle in India. As one of those teachers, James Lawson, an influential black minister who had spent three years as a missionary in India, put it at one of the first SNCC conferences, "By appealing to conscience and standing on the moral nature of human existence, nonviolence nurtures the atmosphere in which reconciliation and justice become actual possibilities" (Lawson, quoted in Carson 1981: 24).

Nonviolent direct action was the main tactic used in the civil rights movement in its movement building phase. It was practiced by both the SCLC and SNCC, thus providing a bridge between the generations. Also important was the practical integration that took place, for example, in the Freedom Summer voting rights campaign of 1964. Then, as well as in many other local organizing efforts, white students from the north joined with blacks to carry out programs of voter registration in southern communities. As with the sit-ins and boycotts and demonstrations that led to sometimes lengthy stays in jail, the voter registration efforts were based on a kind of personal politics where putting your body on the line was a taken-for-granted symbol of commitment. The activist risked danger, injury, and even death in putting his or her beliefs into practice. But she learned self-discipline, even self-knowledge, in the act of exercising a kind of moral courage.

The cognitive praxis also had an organizational dimension, a structure or form that became characteristic of the civil rights movement. First the boycott and the mass meeting in the church – the "spiritual high" of preaching and song – and then the sit-ins and the freedom rides, the more offensive efforts to organize the scene of the nonviolent actions. And then the mass demonstrations and the larger, more all encompassing political efforts to spread the message and to involve people from the entire society in the struggle for equality. What the civil rights movement represented, on this level, was the innovation of organized mass action, an innovation which would carry over into the student movement and then on into the new social movements of the 1970s.

Also important in the process was the "rediscovery" of black history, of black culture, and with it, the reinterpreation of American society. The civil rights movement involved much more than collective behavior and resource mobilization, it involved the crystallization of an area of knowledge: black studies, afro-american history, which first took form in the study groups and the pamphlets of the movement organizations, and then diffused into the universities and eventually into popular culture as well. It involved the expansion of professions and professional roles for movement intellectuals, as the interaction between established intellectuals and movement intellectuals reversed itself in the final phase of the civil rights movement.

The cognitive praxis that can be said to have formed the identity of the civil rights movement was, as with environmentalism, the explicit combination of these cognitive dimensions into a movement praxis. This took place in the early 1960s, and for a few years the interaction of the various dimensions, and not least of the different formulations of different organizations and individuals, provided the basis for the dynamic development of a social movement. The later 1960s witnessed the specialization of the dimensions by professional "leaders," the emergence of extremist positions in the name of "black power" and black separatism, and the gradual dissolution

of the movement's cognitive praxis into fragmented, partial practices of separate organizations. In what follows, we will discuss
some of the movement intellectuals who articulated these interests
and some of the most important contextual factors that affected the
transformation of the cognitive praxis of the civil rights movement
into more particular, professional roles.

### The formation of intellectuals in the civil rights movement

Although a matter of dispute, the origins of the American civil
rights movement are, as already mentioned, usually set in and
around December 1955, when a Negro seamstress refused to give
up her seat on a segregated bus in Montgomery, Alabama (Garrow
1987; Fairclough 1987; Branch 1988). Rosa Parks was secretary of
the local chapter of the National Association for the Advancement
of Colored People, an organization formed as early as 1909 by a
group of established intellectuals (including the black sociologist
W. B. DuBois) to combat racial segregation (Morris 1984). Mrs
Parks had been active in the NAACP's legalist and court-oriented
fight against segregation for many years. Her turn toward direct
action and the following bus boycott – tactics with which what is
commonly known as "the civil rights movement" became identified
– thus represented a personal shift in strategy and orientation. This
act by Mrs Parks was both spontaneous, in that she was angered by
the attitude of a particular bus driver (who had ordered her removed from a bus several years earlier), and one with a long period
of preparation: both Mrs Parks and her local branch of the NAACP
had contemplated just such an action in the hope of setting a new
court case in motion (Garrow 1987). That her action would spark a
mass protest and eventually a new organization with different
strategies and tactics for achieving social change to challenge the
NAACP was of course something they had not foreseen.

Throughout its long history, the National Association for the
Advancement of Colored People had provided a pool of organizational and legal expertise in the fight against segregation in America. Both its centralized, bureaucratic organizational form and its
staff of legal experts expressed its strategy of gradual social change
through changing the laws which governed American society. Built
over the years around a particularity of American political culture
in which the legal system can be used as an arena to promote social

change, the NAACP was geared for legal battles, argued by distinguished experts, not street demonstrations. When, primarily as a direct result of the actions of one of its own members, a mass movement began to emerge, the NAACP was forced into struggle with newly forming groups, and eventually organizations, to define movement goals and tactics along lines suitable to its pre-existing organizational profile. It would come into almost continual conflict particularly with the Baptist ministers, like Martin Luther King, Jr, and Ralph Abernathy; they helped organize the bus boycott which followed Mrs Parks's arrest and eventually formed the Southern Christian Leadership Conference in 1957, which became a focal point of the budding movement and which built around a very different organizational structure and type of movement intellectual.

The strategy of the NAACP favored a particular type of intellectual: the distinguished public figure and legislative lobbyist, personified in executive director Roy Wilkins, a college-educated former newspaperman who had been active in the organization since 1932, when he had been employed to "control" DuBois, who was considered too radical to foster the legal activities of NAACP (Branch 1988: 49–50). Wilkins and the NAACP clashed not only with the direct action orientation of the SCLC but also with the intellectual styles and charismatic qualities of its leaders. It would be more than once that the NAACP would complain of the lack of organization and administration of the SCLC, and eventually other movement organizations, and of having to bail them out of both legal and administrative difficulties.

As noted, however, the success of the bus boycotts led to the formation of a myriad of locally based organizations outside the control of the NAACP. Eventually there developed a need for a more flexible and regionally based umbrella organization to coordinate their activites and to provide both the broader range of vision and the tactical skills necessary to the new mass-based social movement. The SCLC was designed to provide just this flexibility and knowledge. In drawing on a deeply rooted heritage of protest and social reform as well as the oratorical traditions of the black ministry, the SCLC helped create a quite different type of movement intellectual than the NAACP.

In contrast to its hierarchically organized and often austere white counterparts, the black church in the United States is expressive and participatory, encouraging emotional display and group solidarity (Morris 1984; Branch, 1988). Its traditions build around the direct and often emotionally charged contact between participants, where music and song, as well as ministers, play a central role as facilitators. These ministers are often charismatic figures with powerful rhetorical skills which draw upon and interact with the expressive participation of their congregations. Both the style of leadership and the stress on emotive participation thus set the black church in sharp contrast not only to its white counterpart, but more importantly in this context to the rational-intellectual strategies of the NAACP.

When charismatic ministers like Martin Luther King, Jr, mixed the emotive-participatory traditions of the black church with a politicized message, and did so with extraordinary rhetorical skill, it produced the potent basis for new mass-based strategies of fighting racial segregation. It also provided a viable alternative to the expert oriented, slow moving tactics of the NAACP, which in the 1950s had additionally been weakened by concentrated attacks against it by the southern white establishment (Morris 1984). The success of the bus boycotts seemed to reveal to the ordinary black person that direct action, rooted in a common spiritual heritage (as reinterpreted and transformed by respected ministers), could be an alternative to the NAACP. With its base in the black church and its participatory spiritual traditions, the SCLC tapped the basis for a new social movement: a mass of potential activists already structured as a broad community. What was needed then was not so much the formation of a new collective identity as the reinterpretation of an established identity in a more political direction, and a coordinating agency to provide that direction.

As a loosely structured organization, with primarily religious leaders in key roles, the SCLC served first of all to coordinate the activities of the politicized local groups centered in the thousands of black churches spread across the American South. Secondly, or better, concurrently, it provided movement intellectuals and the skills necessary to a social movement in the making. The SCLC sent "movement consultants," speakers, teachers, and organizers to coordinate and plan demonstrations, collect funds, organize workshops, set up clinics and classes, and so on. Its cognitive praxis was grounded on the belief that social change was possible only when individuals participated on a mass scale, changing themselves in the process of their participation, a praxis recognizable from the traditions of the black church. Thus its role was as much "consciousness raising" as it was coordinating and guiding local organizations (Morris 1984: 108).

Here movement intellectuals like Martin Luther King and Ella Baker, the only woman and one of the few non-ministers involved in the top levels of the SCLC, acted as mobilizers of traditions of social protest that contrasted greatly with those expressed by the NAACP (as well as with each other). The charismatic King learned the contents of the "social gospel" tradition of American Protestantism while a student at northern colleges and universities. This school of thought was a religious outgrowth of the Progressive movement led by John Dewey and other intellectuals which, in the 1920s and 1930s, had called for the reform of American institutions, most especially the school system, in the direction of participatory democracy, through "learning by doing." It was through King and other black ministers that this Progressive tradition reached the rural black church, helping to transform the fight against segregation into a mass-based social movement (Branch 1988).

Ella Baker also had intellectual roots in American Progressivism, but in its more pragmatic and nonreligious form. Like King, Baker was reared in the American South in a family of ministers, and educated at its black colleges until she moved to New York City in the 1920s, where she worked as a community organizer concerned with consumer education for the Roosevelt administration's Works Progress Administration (WPA). It was in this context that she encountered the Progressive movement and its ideas concerning social change (Morris 1984: 102; King 1987: 42ff.). Baker helped organize consumer cooperatives in Philadelphia and Chicago, and worked as a journalist before becoming National Field Secretary for the NAACP in the late 1930s. Throughout the 1940s she organized local NAACP chapters in the south and south-western parts of the United States. Thus when she became the SCLC's first associate director in 1958 she had many years of experience as a political organizer. Her type of movement intellectual activity – as temporary organizer and facilitator until local leadership could emerge to take charge – was to conflict almost immediately with the leadership role developed by the ministers of the SCLC, including its president Martin Luther King, Jr.

The civil rights movement thus drew on many sources in constituting its knowledge interests and forming the movement intellectuals who articulated them. Partly through the broad education and experience of Ella Baker, Martin Luther King, and other ministers of the SCLC like Ralph Abernathy, who was trained as a sociologist, the movement opened up to a wider range of intellectual currents than perhaps should have been expected of a local, mass-based movement. Almost immediately after the bus boycotts began, political activists and supporters based in New York and other northern cities made contact with the SCLC. One such movement intellectual who was to prove fateful for the movement was Bayard Rustin, a long-term political activist and expert in the tactics of nonviolent civil disobedience. Along with a few others with similar credentials, Rustin traveled throughout the South offering workshops and advice to local movement groups. Another movement intellectual was Stanley Levison, a New York businessman and political activist of quite another type, who from afar helped organize financial support for the SCLC, giving the budding civil rights movement access to wealthy northern liberals by propagating the virtues of tax shelters and tax-free foundations as sources of income beyond the local churches. Levison, who was in almost constant telephone contact with King, was soon to be instrumental in developing the direct-mail technique of fundraising now so common in the conservative religious movements of the new right (Branch 1988). Both Rustin with his on-the-spot advice and knowledge of the tactics of nonviolent protest and Levison with his financial connections and fundraising skills provided a broad range of experience and contacts to the movement, reaching into the liberal wing of the American establishment, as well as its alternative political culture.[1]

When the first wave of black student protest began with the sit-in demonstration in Greensboro, North Carolina on February 1, 1960, it was Ella Baker who acted immediately, at first on SCLC's behalf, to encourage the emergence of a black student movement based on principles of nonviolent direct action and, most important for her, under local decentralized student leadership that learned by doing.[2] The sit-ins grew at a phenomenal rate: "within two months, thirty-five thousand students were putting themselves on the line. By the end of 1960, seventy thousand students, most of them black but, increasingly, some of them white, had sat-in and thirty-six hundred student demonstrators had been arrested and jailed" (King 1987: 44). Using monies provided by the SCLC, Baker organized a meeting of 200 student delegates to discuss the "non-violent resistance to segregation" in April of 1960, at which she urged the students to remain independent of all established movement organizations, including her own SCLC. The students followed her advice, something which did little to enhance her standing with the organization she represented. When the students created their own umbrella organization later in 1960, the Student Non-violent Coordinating Committee, as a "self-directing" entity, Ella Baker's ideas were central to its self-conception. By 1962 Ella Baker had left SCLC and was functioning, along with the white historian Howard Zinn, as a "senior adviser" to SNCC (King 1987: 48).

Before it was transformed in the late 1960s into a voice of "black power" and separatism, the Student Non-violent Coordinating Committee was an embodiment of a religiously grounded morality that drew on much the same traditions as the SCLC, traditions which were being reinvented through the actions of a new politicized generation. With youthful enthusiasm and religiously grounded spirit, SNCC activists filled the jailhouses of the southern United States with courage and song. It was through the inspiration of ideas articulated by Ella Baker that SNCC could channel and crystallize the wave of sit-ins into coordinated efforts which restirred the civil rights movement after the bus boycotts and marches organized by the SCLC had been more or less accommodated as part of the normal political routines, and thus defused as effective forms of protest.

One central problem faced by all social movements is that of transmitting their energy and ideas from one generation of activists to another, while at the same time combating the gradual incorporation of their protest activities and their activists into established political routines and organizations. As an ongoing political force, social movements must renew themselves, both in terms of supporters as well as in their public presence. As the forms of protest developed by the SCLC began to bring diminishing returns, SNCC was able to organize a new generation, with both energy and innovative tactics. Movement intellectuals like Ella Baker and James Lawson proved essential in this process of knowledge transfer across the generations of protest and protesters. Robert Moses was one of a new generation of movement intellectuals, a recipient and bearer of a tradition.

The quiet patience and moral certainty of Robert "Bob" Moses, SNCC's first field representative in rural Mississippi, came to represent a new type of movement intellectual in this phase of movement building. Moses epitomized the movement intellectual as exemplar. Raised in New York City and educated at Harvard University,

Moses was not only of a different generation than the ministers who guided the SCLC, he brought a different social background into the movement. He was a highly educated, urban northerner, a non-minister, who, like the polished executives who headed the NAACP, contrasted sharply with the poorly educated rural blacks who made up the majority of movement activists, even in SNCC. He was surely one of those sophisticated northerners whom Ella Baker would have separated out in her attempt to allow local leadership to develop. However, the quiet, soft-spoken Moses was no organization man, and he soon developed a leadership style which became identified with SNCC as a whole, at least in these early, more idealistic days. His personal moral courage, which was more philosophically than religiously based, and the common, "countryboy" look he affected, the bib overalls and the roughcut shirt, contrasted sharply with King's brilliant oratory and dandified appearance, as it did with the suit and tie professionals of the central NAACP. Moses articulated an aspect of the movement's identity not so much through his words or ideas as through actions and appearance: he symbolized the basic goodness and courage of "the common Negro." Like Gandhi, he led others through the force of his own convictions, a sense of moral self-righteousness and an apparent lack of fear. Bob Moses anecdotes became part of movement lore to be passed on from one activist collective to another and to form, like the music and freedom songs, an essential element of its collective identity. Moses became both a model and a figurehead for one arm of the civil rights movement, as Martin Luther King, Jr, and Roy Wilkins expressed others.

Robert Moses played a significant role in bridging the gap to the white student activists who were now flowing to the movement, primarily from northern universities, and thus to the wider student movement which would soon emerge. With them he shared not only his youth and social background but also a common intellectual heritage. White university students (at that time at least) could more easily recognize the quotations from Camus that Moses read aloud at organizing sessions than the biblical citations that peppered the speeches of the black ministers. Moses had spent time in a pacifist community in France; as a philosophy student he became well acquainted with French existentialism, read Camus in jail, often citing passages aloud to his SNCC cellmates (Branch 1988: 326; Gitlin 1987: 148ff.). Like Camus's Algeria, Moses experienced in the American South an occupied territory with a terrified, yet submissive population. What could the intellectual with his books and ideas offer in such a situation? This was something Camus had written about and personally dealt with. It was from Camus that Moses developed his often cited phrase that the Negro should be "neither victim nor executioner" (King 1987). From such sources, translated to fit the American context, as well as his experience among Quakers and pacifists, Moses molded a model of the movement intellectual that was to come not only to represent the moral force of the American civil rights movement at an important formative phase of its development but also was to affect the formation and development of the white student movement. Through projects like Freedom Summer in 1964, when white student activists were invited by SNCC to Mississippi, movement intellectuals passed their knowledge and experience on to the emerging student and women's movement in America (McAdam 1988).

Freedom Summer was a plan devised by SNCC to bring white students from elite northern universities to rural Mississippi to help with voter registration. Tactically inspired, the plan built upon the experiences which grew out of the Freedom Rides in 1961, when groups of black and white activists tested new federal legislation concerning integration on interstate public transportation, with violent and dramatic results. However, where the idea of the Freedom Rides originated with the pacifist members of CORE, and attracted the more religious of SNCC's activists, Freedom Summer was more consciously political and tactically oriented. It was designed to bring national media attention to the struggle to enfranchise poor blacks. It was argued that only when well-connected white youths were exposed to the kinds of physical danger that blacks faced every day would the national mass media and, through it, the political establishment act to support the movement's voting rights efforts. Although some SNCC leaders were afraid that bringing such well-educated whites into the movement would threaten the policy of developing local leadership, Freedom Summer was put into effect, with dramatic consequences (McAdam 1988: 38). Within ten days of their arrival, three activists were murdered. The national media flooded Mississippi and voting rights activities became a central focus of movement activities, locally and nationally.

The Freedom rides and Freedom Summer had deep consequences not only for the civil rights movement but also for the student and women's movements which were soon to blossom in America. The shift toward openly political tactics reflected the growing strength of politics over religion as the prime motivating force within SNCC and within the civil rights movement as a whole (Carson 1981). This was a development which would prove to have greater significance than anyone could foresee at the time. What at this point appeared a dynamic internal tension, which contributed to the creative and numerical strength of the movement, soon turned into a source of fragmentation. At the same time, this political turn attracted a wider segment of the youthful population to the civil rights cause, both black and white, something which both watered the seeds of fragmentation and contributed to the formation and development of the new social movements (Evans 1980).

Over the course of their summer in Mississippi the 1,000 primarily white student volunteers gained what was to be the unforgettable experience of total immersion in political activism. They were exposed not only to the violence and danger of America's rural South but also thrust into the arms of a movement. They were directly exposed to SNCC's particular style of working and organizing. Here they found that common intellectual ground that Bob Moses and other of SNCC's movement intellectuals expressed, and the egalitarian and loosely structured organization form that SNCC espoused. These were models that they later transferred on to the new social movements. The anti-authoritarian, antileadership style epitomized by Moses and expressed by Ella Baker was something they would carry back with them to their own universities and to other students (McAdam 1988).

The sense of a social movement as a community of equals fitted well with the participatory democracy themes developed in SDS's Port Huron statement. It also satisfied the desire for direct action. The type of movement intellectual represented by Moses would play an important role in SDS activity throughout the mid-1960s: community organizing in black and poor white neighborhoods and a collective lifestyle which encouraged living what one preached, taking on the modes of dress and speech of those they worked and lived among.[3]

Even while we have stressed the role of students and other groups and professions more normally associated with the term intellectual, it is important to keep in mind that other social groups with little previous experience of intellectual labor took on intellectual tasks in the civil rights movement, and in the process became movement intellectuals. This is the case with all social movements, but it is especially true of the civil rights movement. Here women without formal education, middle-aged and older, played an essential role in setting up and running voter registration workshops, teaching basic literacy skills, creating support networks which made crossing the lines of accepted behavior possible. They taught courses in arithmetic, proper English, and local law. They also manned the offices, providing administrative and moral support just as essential but much less visible than that of their more credentialed colleagues. In this activity they mediated between movement organizations, activists, and supporters, helping to establish the networks of communication and the sense of continuity and collective identity which constitute social movements on a day-to-day basis. Through such activity the movement created its own networks and means of communication, just as it created its own intellectuals.

By 1965, writes Clayborn Carson, "SNCC had become, in the eyes of supporters and critics, not simply a civil rights organization but a part of the New Left: an amorphous body of young activists seeking ideological alternatives to conventional liberalism" (Carson 1981: 175). American presence in the war in Vietnam was being escalated and opposition was growing. Antiwar activities were threatening to replace civil rights as the focal point of oppositional politics, especially among white college students. Where Tom Hayden, the white head of Students for a Democratic Society,had come to Mississipi in 1961 to meet with SNCC organizers, Bob Moses was now travelling to the University of California at Berkeley to speak at antiwar rallies and teach-ins, as "a member of the Third World" (Carson 1981: 184).

This broadening of perspective and radicalization was threatening to other organizations in the civil rights movement. An irreparable rift was occurring between the Student Non-violent Coordinating Committee and the National Association for the Advancement of Colored People as SNCC moved more and more toward the political left. This break was to culminate in 1966 during an impromptu meeting of representatives from the various movement organizations gathered together after the shooting of James Meredith. Having been the first black to enroll at the University of Mississippi in 1962, Meredith had undertaken a solo march through the state to test the new civil rights legislation which guaranteed the protection of citizens on public highways, and he had been shot for his efforts. At this meeting SNCC representatives told Roy Wilkins of the NAACP that it was time for him "to retire and write a book about the early days" (Carson 1981: 207). As the reaction to the civil rights movement grew ever more violent and the inability of the federal government to provide protection became ever more obvious, the call for "armed resistance" gained support. The moral appeals to conscience that characterized the cognitive praxis of the civil rights movement – and which had been common to the SNCC, SCLC, and the NAACP – depended upon a certain attitudinal climate in which even the opposition showed some respect for the rights of the other. The "success" of the movement, however, generated countermovements of racist extremism, which then contributed to a polarization of the knowledge interests of the civil rights movement itself. The legalistic efforts of the NAACP seemed ever more meaningless to activists who had experienced beatings as almost everyday occurrences. The vision of an integrated society which had been the shared worldview of the movement came to be challenged by the competing vision of a separate black nation.

By this time only a few dozen whites were left in SNCC and a new vocabulary was being developed by its energetic and innovative talkers which would further exclude those remaining, terms like "black consciousness" and "whitey" and the custom of calling one another "brother" came into common use (Carson 1981: 215ff.). The idea that race and black identity should be the issue and not brotherhood or racial integration not only made it impossible for whites to work within SNCC, it also further separated the latter from other movement organizations, including the SCLC. By the time Stokely Carmichael became SNCC's chairman in 1966, the positions had hardened and the fragmentation of the movement's knowledge interests had become almost unavoidable.

The first casualties of this new orientation were the white SNCC activists who still remained in the organization. In a series of stormy meetings they were not so much forcibly removed as made to feel outsiders, part of the racial Other, against which the growing black consciousness was forming. With a new worldview as to which race was the prime category of classification, SNCC could hardly afford to have whites in prominent positions. The second casualties were those blacks like Robert Moses who had focused their activism on rural voter registration and developing local leadership. The soft-spoken, rural-based community organizer, exemplified by Moses, who had aimed at securing the trust of local people and helping them to establish their own leadership, was being replaced by a more media-oriented, urban-based agitator, who defined intellectual activity in different terms, providing means of channeling "the anger of the masses." That this anger was seen as racial and not class related was a matter of tension in SNCC, but the Marxist James Forman and the black separatist Carmichael agreed upon the centrality of organized leadership in the movement and thus the centrality of a particular type of movement intellectual activity. The earlier type of movement intellectual had sought dialogue with the Other, both by moral example and by reasonable argument. Cognitive praxis was thus a form of "communicative action" drawing upon a shared basis of experience. When that shared basis was challenged by white extremists and governmental ineffectiveness, another type of movement intellectual could come to the fore. With the call for black power, the cognitive praxis of the civil rights movement shifted to a more aggressive form of "strategic action."

In addition to being racially based, SNCC's new orientation was rooted more in the experiences of younger, urban blacks than those of the rural farmers who had been the focus of its earlier organizing efforts. This shift in focus had consequences for what can be called the third casualties in the internal struggles of the civil rights movement, the other organizations. While the civil rights movement as a whole had shifted a large part of its focus to issues wider than the integration of southern blacks, the SCLC remained rooted in the worldview and the concerns of an older generation of a rural and small-town southern black constituency. It was just this group that SNCC's new orientation was leaving behind for the urban world of a younger generation of blacks whose social identity was perhaps not as anchored in tradition and social structure, and thus more open to the promise of new identities contained in the conceptualization of "black consciousness." The groundwork for this conceptualization had been done by Malcolm X and other militant black separatists, who had already attracted national attention in the early 1960s. It was the bleakness of life and the lack of prospects for poor blacks in the urban ghettos that had formed Malcolm X's worldview; his religion was not the white man's Christianity but the Islam of Africa and Asia (Malcolm X 1966).

Largely through Martin Luther King's efforts and the impetus provided by SNCC and the new left, the Southern Christian Leadership Conference had opened itself to wider social issues, but it would not and could not abandon its original basis in the southern black community. Thus while SNCC went through a painful process of internal conflict which would eventually lead to a new orientation and constituency, the SCLC remained for the most part where it had began. The efforts to move north with the "poor people's campaigns" of the late 1960s ran into opposition from more militant northern black organizations.

Paradoxically, the growing antiwar movement and the increasing realization among blacks that they were paying more than other groups for the costs of the war in Vietnam had the unexpected effect of once again creating common cause between SNCC and the SCLC. Martin Luther King, who had cautiously begun speaking out against the Vietnam war as early as 1965, grew more open and active in his denunciations, to the dismay of the NAACP and other moderate black organizations. When, at a major antiwar demonstration in New York City in 1967, Stokely Carmichael and Martin Luther King embraced before a massive cheering crowd, it was an electrifying moment but a shortlived display of unity. The increasing militancy of SNCC and its program of racial separatism and black power, which were developed in relation to organizing in the urban black communities, were much too radical for the ministers of the SCLC, with their roots in the countryside. Common opposition to the war in Vietnam could not overcome these fundamental differences of strategy, tactics, and generation.

The fragmentation of the civil rights movements did not occur without the active intervention of the established American society, its powerful groups and institutions. The reactions and counter-strategies of the opposition are an essential determinant in the process of development of any social movement. A general polarization had been occurring in American society throughout the mid and late 1960s, as popular support for the war in Vietnam waned and opposition not only gained in strength but also became more confrontational and violent on all sides. The fragmentation of the civil rights movement and SNCC's change in orientation must be seen in light of this general polarization in American society; social forces were pulled to one extreme or the other, leaving vacant the tenuous middle ground of "radical reformism" that the movement had attempted to occupy. Attempts to seat a locally based group at the Democratic party's national convention in 1964 had been defeated at the hands of powerful interest groups, and mounting violence and repression met the movement's organizing efforts in the South. The violence culminated in 1968 in the assassination of Martin Luther King in April and of Robert Kennedy in June, and in clashes between the police and antiwar demonstrators outside the Democratic national convention in Chicago later that year – the middle ground had all but disappeared.

It was SNCC that had most clearly chosen its path on the extreme left. Its Black Power slogan and the black panther logo which had first been used in organizing for voting rights in rural Alabama had now become symbols of an urban-based black radicalism that evoked deep emotional reactions on all sides. When a new Black Panther party advocating armed self-defense was formed in Oakland, California in 1966, it took these symbols as its own, just as it took a willing Stokely Carmichael, who had helped popularize them through his rousing speeches at mass rallies and mass media appearances. When Carmichael was expelled from SNCC in 1969 for his unilateral actions in drawing the organization more and more under the influence of the paramilitary Black Panthers, it was already too late. In the eyes of the established white society, and most importantly its law and order organizations, SNCC was a leading arm of black extremism and violence that was deemed a threat to public safety and treated accordingly. This made the marginalization and isolation of SNCC all the easier. With the Black Panther party, SNCC faced extinction through the violent repression and "dirty tricks" that the FBI and other police authorities could now much more openly apply.

The marginalization of SNCC as just another extremist group was one side of the disintegration of the civil rights movement. The other was the conscious attempt to incorporate more moderate blacks into the institutions and processes of the established society. "Black capitalism" came to be promoted and publicized as an alternative to left-wing extremism, and the real road to black power came to be portrayed as occurring through the election of blacks to positions of power and prominence. The importance of the mass media in effecting this incorporation and professionalization will be discussed in more detail in the concluding section of this chapter.

## The context of communication

As a collective political actor, a social movement must establish itself as a serious and sympathetic agent of change through communication with the general public. It must thus establish itself through communicative action to a wide audience as a force to be taken seriously, while at the same time interacting strategically with opponents. State owned and commercial mass media, as opposed to those internal media established by the movements themselves, are crucial factors in constituting these relationships. The classical movement intellectual, in the role of interpreter and articulator of a collective will – the movement intellectual as ideologist – has in this regard an important part to play. But this part has been greatly altered by changes in the communication networks of modern society. Under modern conditions, constituting the collective identity and sense of common purpose that is central to the making of a social movement is more dependent on the mediation of mass communication than was previously the case. This affects not only the skills involved and the character of the movement intellectuals who apply them, but the very nature of social movements. In this sense, as well as others which have been identified in this book, one may indeed speak of "new" social movements.

More than was previously the case, in contemporary social movements the relationship between movement and public is indirect and technically and professionally mediated. As in modern politics in general, there is less direct contact between individual social movement supporter and the representative leadership. In earlier social movements this relationship between individual and collective, including the public at large, was most often mediated through the printed word produced and distributed by the movement, and the public address. The political tract was most often conceived as a means of making contact, opening on-the-spot communication between activist and potential supporter. That is, the written word often served as a recruiting tool, providing movement intellectuals with a chance to develop and display their verbal and argumentative skills in face-to-face communication. Today the commercial mass media plays a much larger and very different role. This difference is significant in several respects. The mediation of the commercial electronically based mass media has broadened the audiences involved. Audiences are no longer as restricted to activists or supporters as they once were, but have been greatly expanded to include an unknown and largely unsympathetic or at least indifferent mass public. This means that words and deeds must be very carefully chosen, more complicated messages toned down or removed altogether. To be effective, mass mediated messages tend toward being as simple and as little open to misinterpretation as possible, for it is an uninitiated public that is reached, and there is little chance to correct the mistakes an ill-conceived first and perhaps only impression can make.

Mass media interpretation and presentation influences not only a movement's public reception but also its self-understanding and development. Contemporary social movements very early on develop media-conscious strategies and even organizational roles for handling problems of "communication." Mary King, for example, whose memoirs we have had much occasion to use in the course of our analysis of the civil rights movement, functioned as SNCC's "communications coordinator" almost from its inception.

Since media attention is so vital for new social movements in reaching a mass public and getting their message across, activists must use these media and risk in turn being used by them. In our context, this means that the mass media plays an important role in selecting those who will represent the movement to the outside world and in influencing the tactics movement groups and organizations use in their struggle to effect social change. That the media helps make contemporary movements has been well shown by Todd Gitlin (1980) in his study of the American student movement. In dealing with and through the electronic mass media, activists must display an ability for calm self-presentation and verbal quickness before an unseen and unknown audience. In addition, new intellectual roles have been created in the movement, just as they have been in the society at large. Public relations and knowledge related to media techniques have become as much a part of the repertoire of movement intellectuals as they have in society in general, creating a situation where movements draw on a pool of available professional skills and provide a training ground for later professional use as former activists take on new careers in the waning of a movement.

The civil rights movement took form in America at a point of transition, as the electronic media was replacing the print media as the prime force in the communication and interaction between the individual and the collective. It was also a period of transition in the way politics was done in the society. The NAACP, the SCLC, and SNCC were all aware of the importance of the mass media, especially the northern and the national media, newspapers as well as television. However, given the different orientations they expressed and the types of movement intellectual they drew upon and favored, each developed its own media strategy. The media served all three as a means of publicity, of getting the message out to as wide a public as possible, even where the actual content of that message varied according to the specific strategies and tactics of each organization. As the most professionalized and reformist, the NAACP saw in the mass media a force which could be used to influence the elites who controlled the institutions they sought to affect: the courts and the federal government. Being more oriented toward direct action, the SCLC and SNCC had more developed communications networks of their own, both to coordinate the actions of local groups and to formulate an alternative to reportage of events presented in the mass media, especially its local varieties. Of the two, SNCC was the most skeptical of the established media and from its origins consciously worked toward creating its own alternative channels of information and its own movement intellectuals concerned with its production and distribution (King 1987: 561ff.).

In addition to being a way to spread one's own side of the story, the established media served those movement groups engaged in direct action, offering a source of protection against the violence brought against activists by the hostile local white population, including its law enforcement agencies. The presence of newspaper reporters and cameras sometimes acted as a sort of insurance against open violence and in this regard activists were often relieved at the sight of the press during a sit-in or other form of nonviolent demonstration. Of course, the presence of the media could have the opposite effect, inciting rather than preventing physical attacks against protesters. Activists learned very early on to make careful use of the media, in part so as not to be used by it. We can further illustrate these points with a particularly telling example of the effect of the mass media on the making of the civil rights movement.

Because of the presence of television cameras, the live national network coverage, and the desire to present an image of unity and common purpose, the speeches at the 1963 March On Washington were matters of great sensitivity and internal dispute. The text of an address by SNCC's John Lewis was particularly sensitive for it took a more militant stance than was acceptable to other organizations. A phrase about "burning Jim Crow [a shorthand name for segregation] to the ground – nonviolently" was thought especially offensive to the viewing public, which was one prime target group of the demonstration (Branch 1988: 874). Negotiations about the content of the speech continued up to the minute of its presentation, with leaders of white church groups threatening to withdraw their support of the march if the text was not altered. Even as he mounted the podium to face the mass of demonstrators and the millions of viewers across the country, what Lewis would actually say was uncertain, to say nothing of its effects.

The controversy surrounding John Lewis's speech illustrates the tensions created in appearing before a mediated mass audience and why this must be approached in a careful manner so as not to alienate and offend unknown, yet important, potential supporters. In such a situation there is little chance to clarify a complicated issue and even less to make amends should something go astray. This is of course true of any public speech or confrontation, but the risk is multiplied on television.

In addition to reflecting caution related to appearing live before a national television audience, the controversy surrounding Lewis's address also reflected an internal struggle concerning both leadership and choice of strategies in the civil rights movement. As we have stressed throughout, SNCC's focus on locally based direct action and its antibureaucratic stance and structure clashed with the regionally based and charismatic leadership of the SCLC and the professionalism and centralized bureaucracy of the NAACP. Tensions between the organizations were mounting. SNCC's movement style presented as much difficulty in being translated into a mass media event of the March On Washington type as John Lewis's words. SNCC activists had never liked mass demonstrations to begin with, preferring local organizing to displays of unity before the mass media.

This was soon to change, as the "success" of the march revealed the power of the mass media once again, helping to crystallize movement tactics in a particular direction, one aimed more at influencing the established, national elites and institutions than promoting local leadership and change. This shift had the unexpected effect of once again giving whites and white attitudes much more of a central role in movement strategies, something which was to have a great effect on SNCC's own internal tensions and conflicts. At the same time, this shift encouraged the development and prominence of certain movement intellectual styles – those whose rhetorical flair and colorful image were more suitable to a televised message – over others. Even at this point in time, however, before the media enhanced and in that sense encouraged the takeover of SNCC by more colorful advocates of "Black Power" and racial separatism such as Stokely Carmichael and H. Rap Brown, SNCC's ideas about local control and participatory democracy were much more threatening to the established interests and traditions of American politics than either the professionalistic reformism of the NAACP or the church-centered moralism of the SCLC.

While Lewis's address created the most tension and threatened to split the movement at a very crucial stage, Martin Luther King's address at the same demonstration is the most generally remembered of the occasion. This speech illustrates a related point about the centrality of the electronic media for contemporary social movements; it also illustrates the social transitions affecting the continuing development of the American civil rights movement. King, a great public orator and a movement intellectual in the classical mold, was given much more freedom to improvise his speeches than others, and on this particular occasion, as on many others, of course, the results were memorable and the effect on the movement and its public image monumental. King followed the prepared text until he neared the end of his address. With the live audience at a high pitch of emotion and the speech spilling out in a tested pattern of phrases, he suddenly ran out of text. Falling back on his professional training, he began to preach and then spontaneously, yet in full consciousness of his public, the now famous words came out: "I say to you today, my friends, and so even though we face the difficulties of today and tomorrow, I still have a dream. It is a dream deeply rooted in the American dream ...", ending with what are now some of the most recognized phrases of recent American political history, "And when this happens ... we will be able to speed up that day when all God's children, black men and white men, Jews and Gentiles, Protestants and Catholics, will be able to join hands and sing in the words of the old Negro spiritual, 'Free at last! Thank God Almighty, we are free at last!'" (quoted in Branch 1988: 882).

This televised speech and the March On Washington in its entirety lifted the civil rights movement, with Martin Luther King's dream as its symbolic expression, to worldwide attention. Even one of the most direct objects of its political intention, American President John F. Kennedy, viewed the speech on television, witnessing for the first time the power of King's oratory and media presence. As they met directly after the speech to negotiate the formulation of a new civil rights bill, Kennedy greeted King with the words "I have a dream" (Branch 1988: 883).

King's speech and its reception illustrates the power access to the media affords when all goes well. However, it is a particular kind of power, one that can afford access to the highest circles of government and, at the same time, contact with previously unreachable masses. But it is a power that presupposes limited and carefully chosen targets, as well as the great risk of irreparable failure. It requires the careful selection of audiences, skillfully projected images and, as this case well illustrates, the "luck" of the right time and place. It requires, in other words, professional planning and movement intellectuals with particular training and skills, forms of knowledge which are at least as important as the classical oratory of a Martin Luther King, but which, like the legalist strategies and the professional administrators of the NAACP, would direct a social movement in particular directions.

In the early civil rights movement these organizational and administrative specialists seemed to appear spontaneously from the ranks of the local ministry, as well as being provided by the long-established networks of the NAACP. The administrative and fund-raising skills gathered in running small church parishes, entirely dependent upon the active participation and monetary contributions of its members, helped produce ministers with more than the verbal skills that also characterized the southern black ministry. The churches thus offered the movement a pool of organizational experience and knowledge from which to draw its movement intellectuals. These were movement intellectuals of a very special kind, however, having both what can be called professional skills, yet at the same time roots in the community out of which the movement developed. Later other social movements would find it easier to hire unconnected and even uncommitted professionals to perform these necessary services, something which can complicate the very practice of making a social movement.[4]

## Conclusion

The civil rights movement thus offers an interesting case study in the changing conditions for the making of social movements. Occurring at a time of general societal transition, the shift toward a postindustrial economy, where professional services and "knowledge industries" were gaining increasing significance, and where the electronic media were replacing the print media as the prime means of mass communication, it could not but be affected by these developments. Its own cognitive praxis was thus conditioned by the American political culture, as well as by structural shifts in the economy and the societal modes of communication. On the one hand, the knowledge interests took form in relation to the particular emphases of the political culture of American society, most especially the role of the courts and the federal government in effecting – and not effecting – social change, and the importance of religion in politics. In this regard, the separation of American society into a "north" and a "south" with different developmental patterns and different experiences of racial relations was also significant.

The movement's cognitive praxis was also conditioned by structural shifts in the economy and the means of communication. The civil rights movement represents the transition from "old" to "new" social movements. Not only did it provide a bridge and a training ground for young student activists who would go on to play significant roles in later social movements, it also helped revive a sense of political commitment and activism among labor and trade union activists going beyond the job floor and salary negotiations. More important for our context, however, the civil rights movement reflected the shifting focus of consciousness from the material to the cultural as the driving force in the cognitive praxis of social movements. In this regard, the movement was one of the first indications of the coming of postmaterial values, while at the same time warning against the linear, even positivist assumptions that color such concepts. The civil rights movement based itself on a different kind of knowledge than the hegemonic science and technology of the industrial age. Its affirmation of moral courage and personal politics challenged the industrial ethos and pointed to a more pluralistic and democratic society. At the same time, the civil rights movement represented a return to tradition and a mobilization and articulation of ethnic identity which have come to be central ingredients of the contemporary political landscape. As such, the civil rights movement can well be said to have initiated the paradoxical process of postindustrializing through reinterpreting preindustrial ways of life which seems so characteristic of the "postmodern condition."

# 6

# Social movements in context

It has been one of the central arguments of this book that social movements must be understood in their historical context. In this chapter we will put our own theory of social movements into historical context by discussing the structural conditions for the emergence of what we have referred to as old and new social movements. We will try to relate the structural changes taking place in contemporary societies to our cognitive approach to social movements.

## The contemporary context

In sociology, the ongoing transformation of industrial societies has been conceptualized in terms of postindustrialism and postmodernity. The postindustrialists such as Alain Touraine (1977) and Daniel Bell (1974) see, as do many other contemporary observers, a fundamental shift taking place in the international economy beyond an emphasis on manufacturing and even production, toward a service economy and "knowledge" industries. The post-industrial society is one in which knowledge and information are the most important commodities and in which the dominant social actors are those who process information, or what Bell has called "codified knowledge." Their identity is not class-based, and thus the influence of the old class-oriented social movements is weakened. New "postmaterial interests," to use the phrase coined by Ronald Ingelhart in the 1970s, have more and more come to replace the classbound material interests that characterized the industrial order. Of course, there is no more agreement about these arguments than there is about the equally controversial claims about "postmodernity", which focus more on shifts in worldview than in social structure. For our purposes, however, it is important to recognize the underlying societal transition that both conceptualizations attempt to capture. In our terms, a revolution is underway in the cognitive praxis of contemporary societies which has great significance for our understanding of social movements.

On the one hand, or on what we have called in this book the cosmological dimension, there is a widespread questioning of the idea of progress which was the core value of what Jürgen Habermas (1987a) has labeled the "project of modernity." The belief in man and his unlimited ability to recreate the conditions of his own existence, operationalized in science and technology, has, at least since the late 1960s, come under attack. The postmodern cosmology is, at the very least, an ambivalent one, formed by "nuclear fear" (Weart 1988) and the risks of global annihilation, as well as by the environmental and human degradation that dominates the contemporary urban – and increasingly the suburban – landscape. The belief in progress is no longer taken for granted as a shared assumption of social life. And the realization of progress through science and technology has been increasingly questioned. Rather than providing a sense of certainty in a chaotic universe as originally conceived in the secular world view of modernity, science and technology have themselves become a main source of risk and uncertainty in the postindustrial universe (Beck 1986).

The particular technologies that have characterized modernity, from the "wonders" of modern chemistry to nuclear power plants, have also been the main objects of contention in the contemporary period of transition to postmodernity. The new technologies of microelectronics and genetic engineering are of a fundamentally different order. They are not derived from exploiting natural processes as much as decoding them: they do not "use" nature or represent a human intervention in nature, as much as replace it. They are thus termed information, rather than production, technologies. As such, contemporary social movements do not reject these postmodern technologies; rather, they are often proponents of them, using them for their own purposes.

On the organizational dimension, the project of modernity has been based on a strategy of institution building, in which knowledge has come to be produced by certified professional experts in primarily state-supported institutions. The experts and their organizations have held to an instrumental ideal of knowledge and a clear cut demarcation between their world and the political. The cognitive praxis of postmodernity is organized in the image of the private consulting firm, offering its services to the highest bidder and constructing its knowledge according to a relativistic, pragmatic epistemology.

## The routinization of politics

Modern societies are often characterized in terms of differentiated yet integrated *action systems*, in which formal rules and procedures prescribe more and more the avenues of human behavior. Contemporary sociologists speak frequently of "the economic system," "the legal system," "the system of higher education" and so on as shorthand ways to describe the institutionalization characteristic to modernity. Political behavior is seen in the same way. Politics is often defined as that behavior occurring within a distinct action sphere, the political system, where well-defined practices regulate the selection of elites to steer society and administer the distribution of goods and services. Any form of action, individual or collective, or any issue which would challenge these accepted boundaries, must prove itself to be "political" to be worthy of entry into the political arena and the political system. This is as true of social movements as it is of terrorism or other forms of political violence. All such noninstitutionalized action that has the intention of influencing the governing of modern society must struggle to be recognized as legitimate political behavior.

In addition to the way we think of politics in terms of well institutionalized routines, it is also common to think of modern politics as something handled by professionals, and of the political system as a sphere for the application of specialized knowledge. Indeed, in modern society politics has become a career, an occupation one can choose to enter, even at an early age, just as one can choose to be a doctor or automobile mechanic. There exist clear paths to a career in "politics" in all advanced societies, even where the actual content of that path may differ from country to country. In the United States, law and business (and even entertainment) are suitable career paths for politicians; in Europe, university study in economics or government, often combined with activity in student or youth organizations, is a common route to a career in politics.

In sociology, this way of describing the political behavior of contemporary society has been most commonly associated with some form or other of modernization theory (Eisenstadt 1966). Popular with macro sociologists, from Marxists to structural functionalists, modernization theory portrays history in terms of a more or less linear path of development, from undifferentiated, ethnocentric traditional society to differentiated modern society. This model of historical development underlies a good deal of contemporary theorizing about social movements. From its perspective, the collective behavior of social movements is an expression of a need for inclusion, the action of groups, the young, students, ethnic minorities, women, and so on, who feel themselves left out and unrepresented in the routinized procedures of the modern political system. And, from this point of view, it is the job of political professionals to recognize and rectify this situation.

The argument of this book has been against this sort of evolutionary modernism. We believe social movements to be a more or less recurrent phenomenon even in modern, highly organized societies. While it may be possible, as modernization theory suggests, to interpret contemporary social movements in terms of a desire for inclusion by newly formed or conscious social groups, we see something much more fundamental at stake in new social movements. In that they represent challenges to the established routines of "doing politics" new social movements offer the possibility of new projects, new ways of viewing the world and of organizing social life, which is something more than inclusion.

To think of social movements in terms of inclusion is to think in terms of a static world of fixed contexts, in which ready-formed agents struggle to be recognized as legitimate political actors. Our process oriented cognitive approach speaks rather of social movements in terms of the opening of new public spaces in which newly forming groups challenge structured definitions and institutionalized routines of political behavior. The first challenge social movements make is to the established social definitions of what politics entails. In the course of their development, they are often drawn into accepted channels and forced to redefine their conflict and their issues in conventional terms. For, as we have argued, social movements are transitory, impermanent processes which serve to re-collect the political projects of the past into contemporary settings. Redefining situations, opening up new conceptual spaces, and framing new issues in political terms – this is politics in its primary form and is the core around which the cognitive praxis of social movements revolves. This is also the common element bridging the historical gap between "old" and "new" social movements: all social movements originate as attempts to redefine the accepted boundaries of the political.

Redefining politics includes constructing what we have called the Other. The intellectuals of both the old and the new movements have sought to name the people and institutions who wield power and thus are to be opposed: the capitalists, bourgeoisie, the state, the establishment, etc. This is not to deny that significant changes have occurred in the structure of modern societies to affect the actual form and content of social movements and that "new" social movements may be substantially different from "old" ones. A movement does not take form in a vacuum, but rather as Karel Kosik (1976) noted regarding individuals, they "are thrown into an already existing world."

While we agree that substantial changes have occurred in the making of modern societies, these have not so much eliminated social movements or relegated them to the past, as created the conditions for the formation of new social movements. It is time then to offer a more general historical-comparative framework to fill out the cognitive approach outlined in the previous chapters.

## New and old social movements

One central issue in current debates about contemporary social movements concerns whether they are "new" in any more substantial sense. Here we will give an answer to this question by placing the making of social movements into a historical framework of modernity. For the sake of clarity, it is convenient to speak of modernity in terms of interrelated processes surrounding industrialization and democratization: centralization, institutionalization, secularization, and professionalization. The social movements which characterized the late nineteenth century – the labor movement, the early women's movement, the cooperative movement, and so on – were both the cause and effect of these processes; they were for the most part carriers of what has been called the project of modernity.

Spurred by demographic shifts which saw the movement of great masses of individuals from the rural countryside to cities and from individual farms to large factories, these social movements opened new public spaces in which new social and political identities could take form. In this way they mediated the development of a modern, secularized, worldview. To put the matter very simply, in the social contexts created by these social movements, in their meeting halls and gathering places and in the public debate they helped stimulate, new individual and collective identities, as well as ideas and programs, were constituted and tested. Thus the former farmers, craftsmen and laborers who became activists were more than instrumental agents seeking to better their lives in the wave of the changes associated with industrialization; more importantly they were redefining the very basis of their social existence, and in the process redefining politics and reconstituting the political arena. In reacting to industrialization they became "workers" and socialists, as religious country folk were transformed into secularized urban dwellers. On the level of individual and collective identity, these social movements thus helped mediate what classical sociology identified as the transition from traditional to modern society (Eyerman 1990).

One cornerstone of the modern worldview is the notion that the human self is a malleable construct, a notion which emphasizes the creativity of human action; a corollary notion is that society, the foundation of social order, is also a social construction. Both notions challenged traditional ideas about the boundaries between nature and culture, opening up to human intervention areas which had previously been closed. Modernity involves much more than industrialization, the creation of new means of satisfying basic human needs, and the centralization and coordination of the production and distribution of goods. It involves the creation of new views of the social order and the place of the individual within it. The modern world is one in which human skill and knowledge would be the cornerstone of the new social and political order rather than god-given laws or inherited traditions.

In mediating these dramatic changes, the social movements of the nineteenth and early twentieth centuries were organizers and institution builders. The new sense of freedom to create order produced new organizations growing out of voluntary association – trade unions, cooperatives and political parties – which were more than instrumental, as they expressed this new vision of society and the individual. These organizations were seen as the necessary means toward realizing a project, toward either renewing or replacing established patterns of social life along qualitatively different lines.

Central to this realization was refurbishing the state and politics in general. In the new politics, the state was both a means toward actualizing the new visions, an instrument through which to assert power, and an end-in-itself. The state was to be expanded and given new powers. Through the efforts of the social movements and the mediation of the state, individuals were equipped with new "functional" identities; they became workers, students, family members, citizens, and consumers, each "role" implying and entailing its own particular interests and needs, some of which competed and conflicted with each other. In the new state-centered pluralistic societies, each of these interests could potentially be the basis for membership in an association.

At the same time as the state's function expanded, so also did its formally organized structure. The state, as well as the movements themselves, expanded its bureaucratic organization, offering not only structural permanence but also career and employment. This institutionalization brought with it a general societal tendency towards specialization and professionalization, in which social hierarchies formed around differences in knowledge and education, as well as around tasks performed. Specialization was perhaps an unintended consequence of institutionalization, but it had significant effects on internal power relations as well as wider divisions in society. New professional groups emerged which added further to the complexity of the social hierarchy, making more unclear the class lines which had previously formed the major axis of political identity.

The politician and the union representative, among others, thus emerged as occupational categories, often replacing Lenin's "professional revolutionary" among those fully employed with "politics." Doing politics was on the road to becoming a largely professionalized practice, an employment for those with expert knowledge on the one hand, and a routinized and individualized activity on the other, geared to the selection through political parties and standardized voting procedures of elites to steer society. From a form of collective action, politics became routinized individual behavior which could be studied as "science." As individual routinized behavior, politics was made available to the predictive methods of empirical social science in a different way than collective behavior. As politics became administration, political action became political behavior.

The actualization of the "new politics" of the social movements of the late nineteenth and early twentieth centuries created the context in which "new" social movements emerged. The state-centered reformism of the European labor movements helped reform the political order in which new groups were included. Workers and women became accepted categories in the polity. The labor movement was reorganized around social democratic parties; in conjunction with trade unions, they worked to reform society from within through creating a "welfare state," which in addition to being a means for implementing reform also became a employer. In the process these parties became political parties like others, concerned with attaining seats in the parliament. The new politics of the movement was now institutionalized in the political system, routinized in the parliamentary voting process.

In addition to their concern with politics in this narrowed meaning, the social movements of the late nineteenth and early twentieth century were active in what are now called cultural areas as well. They were concerned with issues of education and access to "bourgeois" culture. The labor movements were great supporters of educational reform and the extension of formal educational opportunities to wider sections of the population. Their success in this endeavor had the effect of breaking down the gap between high and popular culture and between the "classical intellectual" and the masses. Thus, while the bureaucratization and specialization had the effect of creating new gaps, the education revolution had the opposite effect.

Education for all "citizens" was a cornerstone of this reform. At first the subject of great conflict and the grounds upon which social movements built, educational reform was incorporated into the aims and policies of the new welfare state and a school "system" was created to include all members of society. This democratization of education was to have a great effect not only on the cultural relations between social classes, but also on the formation of new social movements in the 1960s, as we described in an earlier chapter. Along with the technological developments which produced a new means of communication, the mass media, the democratization of education helped produce a generally available popular culture which helped eliminate the earlier class cultures through which the earlier social movements had developed.

Contemporary social movements are new because they occur at a distinct stage in societal development, involve new actors equipped with different orientations and identities, and aim at achieving quite different ends than old movements. In addition, they take these older movements as part of the Other, a responsible party in the formation of the values and the institutions they react against. New social movements emerge in a new postmodern context in which the central values of the project of modernity as conceived and realized through the active participation of old social movements are challenged. The ideal of progress, intervention into society and nature through science and technology mediated through an expansive state have now become the Other. This is a context that is qualitatively different from the one in which the old social movements originated.

## Social movements in comparative perspective

In addition to setting social movements in their historical context it is also important to look at them comparatively, for the general process just described evolved differently in different national settings, producing a different set of conditions for the emergence of new social movements. One of our concerns in this and other books has been to show how even those movements which are global in outlook and international in organization, such as environmentalism, take actual form as social movements in national settings. The specific character of national political cultures has a direct effect on these social movements, including the structure of their organizations and the issues they take up, and indeed their very identity as social movements. In our studies of environmentalism we were able to show, for example, how the strength of social democratic parties in Sweden, Denmark, and the Netherlands affected the very way environmentalism emerged as a political issue and as a social movement in these countries. The relative strength of social democratic organizations in connection with the strength of what we called alternative political cultural traditions in these societies was a determining factor in whether a social movement around environmental issues emerged at all (Jamison et al., 1990).

Similar differences have been noted in comparative studies of the contemporary women's movements (Katzenstein and Mueller 1987). The influence of political culture can be seen in the relative strength of independent women's organizations, as opposed to those associated with more established political parties, as well as in the definitions and conceptualizations of feminist theory. In some

countries, feminism has developed in opposition to the old movements of the working class, while in others, such as Britain and
Sweden, feminist issues have largely been integrated into more
established political discourses.

These national differences are also striking when one considers
the recent developments in Eastern Europe. The various revolts
against communist rule reflect a common experience of a "different
path to modernity," as well as national differences in political
culture and opportunity structures. As Timothy Garton Ash (1990)
has put it, "In Poland it took ten years, in Hungary ten months, in
East Germany ten weeks: perhaps in Czechoslovakia it will take ten
days."

The emergence of Solidarity in Poland and its transformation
from broadbased social movement to political party and from
underground organization to partner in government follows almost
classic Central European lines. After the intervention by Soviet
troops in Poland and Czechoslovakia in 1968, Poland was among
those Eastern European countries most independent of Soviet
domination. Although not as outspokenly independent as Yugosla-
via on the one side or Romania on the other, its communist party
leaders were permitted to develop a particular "Polish road to
socialism" (Bauman 1989).

After 1968, there continued to exist a comparatively well-
developed alternative political culture consisting of organizations
and networks between intellectuals, students, and workers. When,
in the face of a disastrous economic situation and obvious misman-
agement by party officials, strikes broke out in September 1980 at
the Lenin shipyards in Gdansk and then spread throughout the
country, it was this network that provided access to a means of
communication and intellectual "advisers" to serve as experts in
providing alternative programs and policies (Amsterdamska 1987).
These established intellectuals, however, were only part of the
story as the new public space opened by Solidarity provided an
opening for movement intellectuals to emerge. "One of the most
surprising aspects of the Solidarity episode," writes Zygmunt Bauman, "was the sudden surfacing of thousands of able, educated,
and skillful young men who easily assumed the leadership of a vast
popular movement and reduced the leading professionals among
their sympathizers to the role of counsellors whose advice may be
listened to, but need not be necessarily followed" (Bauman 1989:
64). When this movement was dismantled by the new martial law

and forced underground again, these networks continued to exist. Finally, when a new wave of reforms in the Soviet Union and Poland was given approval, Solidarity moved from underground to opposition party and finally to government. What began as social movement is now an institution.

The emergence of mass protest in Czechoslovakia, East Germany, and Romania in the fall and winter of 1989 took different forms. Faced with more repressive regimes and in the context of better functioning economies (with the exception of Romania, whose mismanaged economy more resembles Poland in this respect), oppositional political cultures had not the years of preparation and organizational structure that existed in Poland. Popular protest appears to have emerged in Romania and Czechoslovakia spontaneously in conjunction with the reform moves in the Soviet Union and in full awareness of what Poland had experienced years earlier. In many respects, Poland served as both positive and negative example: positive in the sense of showing that mass opposition was possible, negative in the sense that mass opposition grew primarily in response to a devastated economy. As it was expressed in Czechoslovakia, "if economic misery were to be the price for political emancipation, many people might not want to pay it" (Ash 1990).

In East Germany what began as an economically motivated demographic movement, a flood of workers in search of better pay and consumers in search of goods into West Germany, ended up as a political revolution. Political change here followed more as the unintended outcome of an unplanned and uncoordinated collective behavior, rather than of a social movement in our sense of the term. But the resulting changes have nonetheless been revolutionary (at the time of this writing, January 1990). As in Hungary and Czechoslovakia, television had played a major role in making visible to East Germans life on the other side of the Wall. Especially in Berlin, but also in most other East German cities, people could watch West German television every evening, providing what has been called an "international demonstration effect," a living image of a form of life they were missing, one lying just out of reach.

But there were other, just as powerful, internal pressures as well. Like other Eastern European countries, including the Soviet Union, East Germany was in a state of economic crisis: the flood of economic refugees, the primarily younger skilled workers were not only fleeing to West Germany, they were also fleeing from the disastrous conditions of their own country. Here the Soviet Union had provided the example of what was lacking in their own country: radical economic and political reform from above. The Soviet leader Gorbachev's program of glasnost and perestroika, liberalization from above, the attempts to reform the stagnation connected with a centrally steered economy and an overblown defense apparatus provided East Germans with a model of what was also possible for them. The East German party officials however did not see things the same way. As massive public demonstrations were being planned in Leipzig after a state visit by Gorbachev in October 1989, the East German officials were preparing police and military actions against them. However, when approximately 70,000 nonviolent demonstrators appeared in Leipzig on October 9, they were permitted to peacefully demonstrate their protest against the government. Like the flood of refugees, this successful demonstration spurred others and suddenly a giant reversal had occurred: it was now the people who were acting and the party that was reacting. Party leadership was forced to resign and new oppositional parties were permitted into the legitimate political arena. The lines between politics and society had been redrawn.

## The oppositional intellectuals

Students played a central role in all the Eastern European movements, as they did in China. They were, in our terms, movement intellectuals making politics personal, putting their bodies on the line. They had the time and the desire to defy the routines of daily life, for their daily lives were not yet routinized. Partisan intellectuals were significant also. In Poland, KOR, the committee for the defense of workers, played a significant role in helping turn the spontaneous strikes at the shipyards of Gdansk into Solidarity and in seeing to it that Solidarity did not become an ordinary (even in the Western sense) trade union. It helped continually raise the political stakes of the movement.

In Czechoslovakia, these partisan intellectuals were of a different sort. First, there were the classical intellectuals turned publicly dissident with the signing of Charter 77 and their underground press activity. After the outbreak of mass demonstrations following the beating of students on November 17, 1989, these intellectuals formed a group of veterans in the Civic Forum, a loose

organization which emerged to coordinate events and produce statements and which eventually formed the basis of the new government
after the collapse of the communist regime 14 days later. But another
even more significant group of movement intellectuals emerged
from an unexpected (from the point of view of established theories)
source: actors. The nation's theaters were at once transformed into
giant meeting halls as plays were interrupted with political speeches
and debate. This middle-class, educated public spurred not only the
mass movement but also the creation of movement intellectuals. It
is therefore appropriate that the current president, Vaclav Havel, is
a playwright.

As we have noted throughout this book, a central aspect in the
formation of a social movement is the constitution of the Other
against which it is to react. This process was complicated in Eastern
Europe. Again Romania is the exception, in that the obvious other,
the Communist party and its government, soon collapsed in the
face of such massive opposition and with the benign neglect of the
Soviet Union. As Ash expresses it, "To say 'the government', for
example, would be wrong, since in such systems the government
did not really govern: the Party did, or some mixture of the Party,
the police, the army, and the Soviet Union" (Ash 1990: 44). It was
not only difficult to locate the Other, it was difficult to negotiate
with persons who could represent it. Thus the whole concept of
power inherited not only from Marxism through Lenin but also
with social movement theory in general had to be modified in a
more Foucaultian direction: power was everywhere and nowhere.
The crowds just stayed in the streets until the Other fell away.
There were no buildings to seize, no palace to attack, no capitalists
to dispose of, no Red Army to fight.

Significant, too, in all the movements was the mass media: the
foreign press to communicate with The World, as it was expressed
in Poland and Czechoslovakia; and television to communicate with
the local population beyond those assembled in the mass demonstrations. In countries where for years the mass media had
functioned as propaganda apparatus for the ruling establishment,
television stations were among the first institutions fought for and
seized by the new movements. In Romania, where for a time
fierce fighting went on between movement forces and those of the
deposed dictator, live impromptu TV broadcasts by a range of
dissident figures, movement intellectuals, informed both the national population and the world of the course of events.

In Romania the Other was easy to define. What was more difficult was to define the movement. Without the experience of opposition and the years of preparation and organization, as in Poland, and even without the minimal preparation in Hungary and Czechoslovakia, the protest took place mostly in a negative sense, in the actual military struggle against the regime. When the regime was defeated the real struggle to form the movement began.

## On the future of social movements

What these recent events mean for the future of social movements, it is, to say the least, too early to say. How quickly the "movements" of the Eastern European countries are transformed into new political parties and governmental elites depends on both internal and external events. From our perspective, the events in Eastern Europe indicated the fundamental role of social movements in sociohistorical change. It is therefore of some importance to distinguish those countries, such as Poland and Czechoslovakia, where mass protest became articulated by movement intellectuals into a movement identity, from other Eastern European countries where oppositional forces have not developed an independent cognitive praxis.

For the Western European countries, the events in Eastern Europe signify a decisive change in the relations between the old and the new social movements. The 1980s have brought a fundamental political challenge to the old social movements of the working class, institutionalized as social democratic parties and, in some places, wielding state power. The historical project of modernity which has characterized the old social movements can be expected to decline in significance in the social movements of the 1990s and beyond. What those projects will be is something we leave to the futurologists. Perhaps we have at least provided a conceptual framework that can be useful in their speculations.

# 7

# Conclusions

We began this book with a diagnosis of the contemporary condition of the sociology of social movements. Starting with the familiar dichotomy between European and American approaches, between resource mobilization and identity theory, we tried to explain why the field was fragmented. We explored the contexts in which the various approaches had developed, both in terms of intellectual history and in terms of political culture. We showed that there are both internal scientific reasons for disagreement, as well as political and social conditions which have led sociologists in different directions.

Such a situation need not be debilitating: as we have tried to show in this book, crisis can often be a source of inspiration for new developments in social science. We have had occasion to discuss several attempts to resolve the conflicts between the divergent approaches in the study of social movements with new concepts and methods. And it is in such a spirit of reconciliation that this book has been written. Much like the movements we have studied, we have seen our task in this book to open up new conceptual spaces and provide a set of new assumptions for social analysis.

Our cognitive approach to social movements attempts to move beyond the fragmented or partial approaches currently dominating the academic marketplace to a new kind of synthetic conceptualization. By focusing on social movements as cognitive actors, and examining, in some detail, their intellectual activities, and, more broadly, their contributions to human consciousness, we have come to develop a fundamentally different position than our colleagues. Rather than carving out a special sociological niche, a new subfield of social movements, we have tried to locate social movements within a historically and politically informed social theory of knowledge.

Building both on critical theory and on the sociology of knowledge, we have uncovered something rather important about the ways in which societies are constructed; we have made social movements visible in the social process of knowledge production. The forms of consciousness that are articulated in social movements provide something crucial in the constitution of modern societies: public spaces for thinking new thoughts, activating new actors, generating new ideas, in short, constructing new intellectual "projects." The cognitive praxis of social movements is an important, and all too neglected, source of social innovation.

Our approach is a process of re-collection, recombining what are now analytical fragments into a new synthesis and remembering the experiences of past movements while reflecting on their cognitive "results". Our reading of social movements is based on historical reconstruction and on sociological reinterpretation applying the contextual methods of science studies to a new and wider societal context. Only by moving backward to the contextual sources of the current situation have we been able to overcome the fragmentation that afflicts the study of social movements. We resolve the contradiction by seeking a forgotten – or at least neglected – commonality between the opposing schools of thought. That commonality is what we call cognitive praxis.

In spite of their apparent differences, what the contemporary approaches have in common is an interest in knowledge. For resource mobilization, the cognitive practices of social movements are seen in terms of shifting orientations and organizational profiles, issue clusters or sectoral problems. Knowledge is seen as an organizational attribute; it is the particular organization within a social movement that makes knowledge useful as an instrument for mobilization. Identity theorists are interested in consciousness and ideology; for them, movements are seen both as processes of collective identity formation and as social actors struggling to define history. The one role has tended to be reduced to a semiotic inspired social psychology of symbolic protest (Melucci), while the other has been abstracted to a post Marxian discourse of postmodern ideologies (Touraine, Gorz, Boggs). As a result, the specific contributions of social movements to social processes of knowledge production – and the specific cognitive praxis of specific movements – receive little if any notice.

Much of our analysis in the preceding chapters has drawn on particular studies of particular movements: what we referred to in chapter 1 as the particularist school of social movement sociology. Indeed, our approach can, in many ways, be considered a rereading of these particular accounts. But it has been a special kind of rereading, one explicitly informed by social theory. Most sociologists and historians studying particular movements have told stories, that is given a narrative account of social movement formation. In Doug McAdam's phrase, they have seen social movement as "political process." In most accounts, knowledge production has not been a topic of central importance. But the dimensions of cognitive praxis have nonetheless been there, and in many ways the thick narrative descriptions of actual movements have provided us with the raw material for our own cognitive approach. We have sought to draw from the histories of particular movements conclusions about the social processes of knowledge production. We have both generalized and theorized the findings of the students of particular social movements.

By reading social movements cognitively, we have attempted to redirect social theory away from the abstract universals of language, structure, action, and system back to the contexts in which human beings construct their social reality. In seeing social movements as cognitive praxis, we have tried to show that "society" is continuously being recreated through complex processes of interaction and innovation in particular contexts. Our cognitive approach aims to use empirical material to make a contribution to ongoing theoretical debates in sociology. Like other actor-oriented social theorists, we see social change in terms of historical process, but we want to claim for that process of history-making a "deeper" philosophical significance. As such, we want to contribute to discussions about the relations between knowledge and society and how social context affects the development of human knowledge. By making social movements visible and by uncovering the mechanisms through which social movements create new historical identities, we have identified an important missing link in the chains of determination and conditioning that have long bewildered the philosophers and sociologists of knowledge.

The value of our approach derives in large measure from the fact that it has grown out of a dialogue between the authors, one of whom is schooled in critical social theory, the other in historical sociology of science. It was the combination of our two traditions that made it possible for us to counteract the tendency toward fragmentation that appears to dominate the sociology of social movements. Indeed such fragmentation seems to be characteristic of social science in general. The "coming crisis" of Western sociology that Alvin Gouldner (1970), in the wake of the student revolts of the 1960s, was one of the first to foresee has been our mutual starting point. We have sought to respond to the crisis that has indeed come, and not just to Western sociology, through synthetic reflection, by critically reviewing and recombining the legacies that brought on the crisis.

By the 1960s, when Gouldner was writing his diagnosis, the study of social movements had been incorporated into sociology as a specialty area that seemed to have little relation to broader questions of theory and history. As society had been turned into a social system free of ideology and contradiction, social movements were banished either to the dustbin of history, to the deviant behavior taking place on the margins of society, or to the interest organizations and social democratic "movements" that had replaced social activism in many countries. As such, sociology was unprepared for the new wave of social movements that began in the late 1950s and is still with us today.

The ensuing new social movements have been difficult to conceptualize for sociologists. As we show, the earlier traditions have been rediscovered and, in some cases, fundamentally modified, but the old differences remain. It is only those analysts working from within the perspectives that have evolved out of the new social movements themselves who have been able to articulate their historical significance and underlying meaning. Our conceptualization is a product of the collective process of remembering that has taken place within the context of the new social movements. On the one hand, the movements of the 1960s and beyond have returned to the early Marx and the vision of a socialist humanism, reviving a critical approach to social science. On the other hand, the new social movements have problematized scientific knowledge and its social roles and functions, reconnecting to earlier challenges to the hegemony of science and technology both by social movements and romantic artists.

These two critiques attacked the "one-dimensional thought" of industrial society (Marcuse 1964) from two different directions – the one political, the other academic. And they have tended to go separate ways. They have rarely been combined, except within the new social movements themselves. Our notion of cognitive praxis draws on both types of critique in attempting to provide a framework for understanding the significance of social movements. With critical theory, we see social life as consisting primarily of processes of meaning-filled action, as praxis; with the critics of science, we see that praxis as having relevance for epistemology, that is for determining what is to be considered "true" knowledge and how that knowledge is to be attained.

We have attempted to operationalize these issues by referring to the knowledge interests of social movements, or the dimensions of cognitive praxis. What earlier critical theorists called consciousness is not an individual possession, determined by structural relationships, but a form of identity, a kind of knowledge that is formed in the context of a social movement. Our attempt to characterize cognitive praxis is a way to specify – and even more crucially, contextualize – the making of consciousness; consciousness, we claim, can be broken down into its component parts and related explicitly to the emergence of new forms of knowledge production.

Marxists have difficulty moving beyond the cognitive praxis of the nineteenth-century movements; for them, class identity is still the fundamental kind of identity, even when modern societies are no longer divided, in any meaningful way, along class lines. Structural functionalists have difficulty seeing beyond the interests of the system as a whole. There is no identity other than that derived by structure and function. It is really only historians studying particular movements – E. P. Thompson (1966) studying the English working class, Charles Tilly (1978) studying contentious events in the eighteenth century, Charles Webster (1975) studying the Puritan revolutionaries of the seventeenth century, Taylor Branch (1988) studying the civil rights movement – who have been able to see that consciousness is itself a historical construction. But they have not wanted to take that further sociological step and generalize their specific findings to other movements in other times and places.

The particular way in which social movements develop is shaped by political culture and historical conjuncture, and cognitive praxis and movement intellectuals are movement specific. But we have tried to find beyond the specifics certain general processes that characterize quite different types of social movements. Our case study on the American civil rights movement tried to put our concepts, which we had originally applied to environmentalism, to the test: can one read a social movement which is as emotional and religious as the American civil rights movement in a cognitive way? Is it meaningful to try to identify cognitive praxis and intellectual practices in such a movement? Obviously, it is up to the reader to decide if our reading added anything fundamental to the voluminous literature on the subject. In our case study, as indeed throughout the book, our task has not been to add new information so much as to put available "facts" into new light. Ours has been the hermeneutic aim of deepening understanding: recollection.

Our argument is that social movements articulate new historical projects by reflecting on their own cognitive identity. In formulating their common assumptions, developing their programmatic presentations of themselves to the rest of society, in short, by saying what they stand for, social movement activists develop new ideas that are fundamental to broader processes of human creativity. In the conceptual spaces that are constructed by social movements, we have identified a cognitive praxis along three dimensions. First and most centrally, there is a cosmological dimension: social movements bring societies back to the big questions of what is man? what is nature? what is history? Social movements develop worldviews that restructure cognition, that re-cognize reality itself. The environmental movement discovered a new territory for social activity which necessitated the development of new scientific theories and methods of investigation. The civil rights movement carved out a new path to self-knowledge, and re-cognized American society as fundamentally unjust, combining religious and legal consciousness into an integrated "social gospel." But there are also organizational and technical innovations that draw on the new ideas about knowledge that emerge in the public spaces of social movements. In our day, the environmental and feminist movements have led to the emergence of whole new scientific fields and branches of technology; and in the nineteenth century, social movements opened up entirely new "territories" for scientific investigation that had previously been dominated by religious or metaphysical thought. Generally speaking, social movements provide a challenge to the dominant assumptions of the social order, making problematic the self-image of societies, and with it, the conceptualizations of social science that contribute to that self-image. They also provide spaces for new conceptualizations and organizational forms to develop, serving as social laboratories for experimenting with new forms of cognition.

The cognitive praxis of social movements is an important source of new societal images and the transformation of societal identities. Revolutions are the most extreme example of this, but all social movements, by definition, bring about some kind of identity transformation. On one level, they do this by setting new kinds of problems for societies to solve, by putting new issues on the historical agenda. On another level, they do this by proposing new cosmologies, or "values" which enter into the ethical identities of individuals. And on a more institutional level, they do this by generating new "types" of professional intellectuals, who, as it were, carry the cognitive praxis of the movement on into the larger society.

Our concept of movement intellectuals transforms Gramsci's insight into the class formation of intellectuals into a more general point about intellectual formation. By focusing on the intellectual activities that are carried out within movements, we tried to show how social movements provide a social laboratory for the testing of new social roles. But those roles do not emerge ready made; rather they are created in the process of turning local protests into social movements. Movement intellectuals draw on established intellectual contexts, but the established tradition must always be reinterpreted and adapted to the needs of the movement. It is not, as Lenin insisted, the intellectual who brings consciousness to the movement: that was the central fallacy of Stalinism. It is rather the case, as the young Lukács insisted, that intellectuals become conscious within the context of a social movement. In a very real sense, the social transformations that are currently taking place in Europe bear eloquent witness to the formative role of social movements in new intellectual practices. The future of Europe, it seems, is in the hands of recombined ideas and recombining intellectuals who have been formed in the process of social struggle. The reformists of Eastern Europe and the postmodernists of Western Europe are acting on the projects that have been articulated in social movements. An understanding of those projects, in their own terms, as dimensions of cognitive praxis, can thus be an important, even crucial task for social theory. We hope that this book has made some contribution to fulfilling that task.

# Notes

## Introduction

1 The one exception to this general tendency in the range of textbooks in the field, and the approach which comes the closest to our own, is that of J. A. Banks (1972). In what is a stimulating long essay rather than a systematic presentation of the field, Banks argued against the then dominant marxist and structural functional approaches to the study of social movements and proposes the alternative as one which views them as innovative forces for social change. While we share this orientation, we differ from Banks in our focus on contextual and comparative analysis.

## Chapter 1   Social movements and sociology

1 In addition to the works mentioned on collective behavior, see R. E. Park, "Collective behaviour," in *International Encyclopaedia of the Social Sciences*, 15 vols, London: Macmillan, vol. 3: 631–3; Richard T. La Piere, *Collective Behavior*, New York: McGraw-Hill, 1938; Hadley Cantril, *The Psychology of Social Movements*, New York: John Wiley, 1962 (originally published in 1941); David L. Miller, *Introduction to Collective Behavior*, Prospect Heights, Ill.: Waveland Press, 1985. Blumer elaborates his earlier work on crowd behavior into a theory of social movements in "Social movements" see Blumer 1951: 199–220.

2 Those collective behaviorists of structural-functionalist inclination are similar in this regard. However, given the more pronounced and aggressive empirical orientation of Anglo-Saxon social science, they never dared make these connections as explicit as their European colleagues.

3 Weber's political positions and the ambiguity he felt toward the labor movement and working class of his time are well spelled out in

Beetham (1974) and Mommsen and Qsterhammel (1987). Both Beetham and Mommsen give an interesting portrait of the multi-sided relationship between Weber and the radical, movement-oriented, Roberto
Michels.

4   This "organizational approach" was originally proposed not as an
alternative to collective behaviorism, but rather as a way of "bridging
the gap" between collective behaviorism and organization analysis (see
Zald and Ash writing in 1966, in Zald and McCarthy 1987: 463).
Central to this debate is the very idea of a social movement: are social
movements strategic actors who can be judged as "successful" or not in
conventional terms, or are they something else? For resource mobilization theorists, social movements are organizations which, like other
organizations, express certain aims/goals which they attempt to achieve
by applying their resources (capital, manpower, ideas, etc) in more or
less effective ways. The question then, as far as organization and
leadership is concerned, is which organizational form is the most effective in mobilizing and applying resources. Gamson (1975) for example
has challenged the Weber-Michels model in attempting to show the
effectiveness of certain types of bureaucratic organization, arguing that
those social movements which were the most "successful" were those
which adopted just these types of organizational form.

5   Already in the late nineteenth century, among the founders of the
social democratic parties in Germany, Russia, and elsewhere, "scientific socialists" sought to distinguish their own movement from their
anarchist, syndicalist, and/or utopian competitors. This is discussed,
among other places, in Kolakowski 1978.

6   England is an interesting case. On the one hand, there was much
turmoil on the campuses and great interest in the events in France and
the United States, yet a distinct student movement never really took
form. This be can partly be explained by the hegemony "old" left
organizations and ideas held in the oppositional political culture. Like
Sweden, England had a relatively strong labor party which also had its
organizations on the university campuses, in the student unions and
thus was in a position to funnel "student" protest along lines more
congenial to class analysis. In addition, also like Sweden, the higher
education system in England did not suffer from the same kind of
overextension as in those countries where the student movement was
strongest: France, Italy and the US (Rootes 1987). What distinguishes
Sweden from England, where a "new left" student movement did exist
for a short period, was the strength and character of the opposition to
the American involvement in the Vietnam war. In fact, it appears that
it was the student organizations that pushed Swedish prime minister
Olof Palme to his much publicized apposition to the war. Nothing
comparable occurred in England.

7   Besides Lipset (1967) there were others who challenged the "aliena-

tion" thesis about the new movements. One was Frank Parkin (1968), whose study of CND supporters explicitly set out to test the view that activists were young and "alienated." He found that for the most part they were neither.

8  This difference, it is suggested, as well as many others between American and European analysts of the new social movements, are well illustrated in the articles in the first volume of the series (Klandermans et al., 1988). It is striking how each author of these collected articles develops almost independently, it seems, his/her own terminology for approaching the subject. It appears as if the case study attitude, so dominant throughout the social sciences, has come to afflict the study of social movements in that sociologists develop their explanatory frameworks from their own cases and not by reference to a more general or consensual discourse.

## Chapter 2  Social movements as cognitive praxis

1  This was the specific ambition of Georg Lukács in *History and Class Consciousness*, and of Karl Korsch in *Marxism and Philosophy*, both published in 1923, while the authors were still active revolutionaries in Hungary and Germany respectively. At the time, Stalinism had not yet come to dominate the Marxist movements, and a variety of Marxisms were presented by "movement intellectuals" like Lukács and Korsch. In Russia, Bukharin and Trotsky, among others, were developing alternative conceptions of knowledge, and in other European countries, Marxist intellectuals like Anton Pannekoek, Antonio Gramsci, Ernst Bloch, and many others were challenging many of the scientists' assumptions of the theorists of the prewar Second International. Also worth mentioning, in this regard, is the development of alternative anarchist and syndicalist traditions in the socialist movements of the times, inspired by the writings of Kropotkin, Bakunin, Malateesta, and others.

2  Thus, the Swedish antinuclear movement succeeded in the strategic goal of limiting the expansion of nuclear energy in Sweden while failing to challenge the dominant belief system that nuclear energy embodied. Without sufficient space for the articulation of its knowledge interests, the protest against nuclear energy never became a social movement. Its arguments were derived from, and absorbed into, the established political and institutional culture. It was only when the environmental movement adopted established forms of political behavior, that is, when it was incorporated as a new political party or as a new multinational pressure group (Greenpeace) that its message could begin to have some effect.

## Chapter 4   Social movements and their intellectuals

1   Gramsci's original formulation in the *Prison Notebooks*, was "All men are intellectuals, one could therefore say; but all men do not have the function of intellectuals in society," (Gramsci 1971: 121).

2   One of the main explanations that has been offered for the effectiveness of the Danish antinuclear movement, for example, was the ability of the national secretariat to present different antinuclear arguments for different audiences. This ability to translate arguments from one social context to another is characteristic of antinuclear movement intellectuals in most countries. The antinuclear movement required not merely members, or active support, but at least the tacit approval of a majority of the population. In this respect, the intellectuals of the antinuclear movement can be considered embodiments of the "interpreter" intellectual as opposed to the "legislator" which Zygmunt Bauman has seen as typical of postmodern society (Bauman 1987).

3   These spaces are not dissimilar to the opportunity structures of resource mobilization or to the new public spaces of Jürgen Habermas (1989) in which new forms of collective identity are tested out. But what such theorists do not see is the activity within those structures and spaces, and the types of movement intellectuals who constitute those spaces through their cognitive praxis.

   Movement intellectuals are invisible to those whose thinking is encased in traditional models of organization, and who focus only on the instrumentality and/or symbolism of cognitive praxis

   What people do when they "do" a social movement is something which ethnomethodologists should be interested in. Given the general orientation of this field of sociological inquiry, however, the focus would most probably be on the social construction of the movement by actors, including those we have called movement intellectuals, and the presentation of the movement to and for others; the way, for example, activists "create" the movement as a means of pressuring authorities into compliance by claiming to speak for a largely unknown and unseen mass of supporters in their dealings with established authorities.

4   There were obviously precursors to the "movement intellectuals' who emerged with the labor movement, and it is a matter of dispute whether we want to call them intellectuals or not. Our point here is merely to stress the formative role that the social movements had on the very conception of intellectual activity. And even more to the point, we want to argue that the social movements of the nineteenth century were crucial on providing the social space for the constitution and the creative role articulation that is now conceptualized as intellectual practice.

5   The question of truth and true knowledge as the outcome of common struggle and political activism cannot ignore the tension between the strategic needs of the movement and the more communicative needs of truth. The case of journalism is interesting in this regard. Karl Radek once quoted Leo Jogiches, the movement intellectual and lover of Rosa Luxemburg, to the effect that "each written line must serve a concrete purpose ... revolutionary journalism is not literature but a battle with pen in hand. He showed us that a revolutionary newspaper is not a compilation of news but a fighting force whose elements, created by different people, serve one concerte purpose" (Ettinger 1987: 124). Here the question of truth is clearly shown as secondary to expedience and the need to organize and carry out a strategic struggle.

6   One should immediately say, however, as we will illustrate in the next chapter with an example from the American civil rights movement, that the centrality of television to modern politics in general and to contemporary social movements in particular has had the ironic effect of reviving the distinction between the movement leader and the faceless masses.

7   Here and in later tracts the university was painted as a symbol of a new type of society where knowledge would be a source of power and privilege and the intellectual a laborer caught in a giant knowledge producing machine. Later this generalized program for action would be given a more theoretical, and ideological, sophistication and a left-wing twist in "new working class theory" which built upon the emerging conflicts at American universities and the rejection the role given intellectual labor in the new postindustrial "knowledge society." Students were here portrayed as workers in knowledge producing factories, with common interests with other workers producing other kinds of goods in other factories, rather than a privileged elite. Both the Port Huron statement and the "Port Authority Statement," as wry New Yorkers called the first American articulation of new working class theory (the Port Authority being the name of New York City's central bus terminal), were carried out by "intellectuals" in the classical manner: "movement-intellectuals" putting into words what they hoped many others were feelings.

8   In an earlier speech entitled 'The student and the total community,' Al Haber, the first president of SDS, called for the expansion of the role of the student to one that "involves a commitment to an education process that extends beyond classroom training. It involves also the attainment of knowledge and the development of skills and habits of mind and action necessary for responsible participation in the affairs of government and society, on all levels – campus, community, state, national, international' (Miller 1987: 49).

9   Melucci is particularly good in stressing the formative processes of

collective identity. Most other theorists of social movements deal with this problem as one of organization, stressing the need for institutionalized roles and order (e.g., Gamson) rather than the processes of interaction in the production and maintenance of collective identity.

This centrality of the processes of collective will formation or collective identity is what distinguishes a social movement from a pressure group, which is formally organized and relatively certain of its goals and the interests it represents. Classical movement intellectuals play almost no role in the cognitive praxis of a pressure group, being replaced by the holder of specialized knowledge: the expert.

10   We will not go into the question of whether or not the CND is a social movement or a pressure group. For a history of the CND and a comprehensive study of its membership and goals see Paul Byrne (1988).

### Chapter 5   A case study: the American civil rights movement

1   Both Rustin and Levison were soon to be liabilities. As the movement grew in political significance, the American political establishment was forced to take notice. During the Kennedy presidency, the Federal Bureau of Investigation (FBI) under the leadership of J. Edgar Hoover set out to monitor the activities of its leaders, most especially Martin Luther King. One long-term aspect of American political culture is simultaneously the fear of "communism" and its use in the political game of discrediting opponents. As the government agency charged with internal police affairs, the FBI was often put in service as a watchdog agency investigating subversion, gathering information that was often extremely damaging and thus extremely useful in political combat, a role which Hoover apparently relished. Both Bayard Rustin and Stanley Levison had left-wing political sympathies, the latter having allegedly associated with the American Communist party in his youth. In addition, Rustin was homosexual. The combination of left-wing sympathy and nonorthodox sexuality is lethal in American politics and Hoover spared no time or energy in attempting to use the connections between King, Rustin,and Levison to his advantage. For details, see Garrow 1987 and Branch 1988.

2   After giving a speech to a large crowd of students in 1960, Ella Baker divided the group into smaller sections for discussion. In doing so, she had the northerners present divide into a separate group because "they were more experienced than the southerners and their ability to articulate themselves would have been intimidating to the southerners" (King 1987: 45). Her ideas were later to be adopted by other student

movements and then the women's movement, through the participation of many white students in SNCC.

3   For the late 1960s this was more or less typical movement intellectual behavior and in some respects represents the rediscovery of the partisan intellectual style of the nineteenth century: déclasse's intellectuals taking on working-class habits of dress and speech and in the process constructing an ideal image of "the worker" which was to prove to be a powerful ideological weapon in the internal warfare of the "class struggle." This is something also that intellectuals articulate: an ideal image of their historical subject. The worker who could do no wrong, the good negro, the native American, or the pure primitive, natural man: all have been articulated as ideal types in the service of mobilization by movement intellectuals.

4   This is of course nothing new to contemporary social movements. The labor movements of the early part of this century faced similar options and at least in the United States devoted a great deal of energy debating the relative worth of hiring noncommitted professionals or training their own committed activists in the professional skills necessary to running a modern movement. The opposite problem also emerges: the bungling movement amateur trying to do a professional job.

# References

Amsterdamska, O. 1987: Intellectuals in social movements: the experts of "Solidarity." In S Blume et al. (eds), *The Social Direction of the Public Sciences*, Dordrecht: Reidel.

Aronowitz, S. 1988: *Science as Power: Discourse and Ideology in Modern Society*. Minneapolis: University of Minnesota Press.

Ash, T. Garton 1990: The revolution of the magic lantern. *New York Review of Books*, January 18.

Bahro, R. 1984: *From Red to Green*. London: Verso.

Banks, J. 1972: *The Sociology of Social Movements*. London: Macmillan.

Bauman, Z. 1987: *Legislators and Interpreters*. Cambridge: Polity.

 1989: Poland: on its own. *Telos*, 79, spring.

Beck, U. 1986: *Risikogesellschaft: Auf dem Weg in eine andere Moderne*. Frankfurt: Suhrkamp.

Beetham, D. 1974: *Max Weber and the Theory of Modern Politics*. London: Allen and Unwin.

Bell, D. 1962: *The End of Ideology*. Cambridge, Ma.: Harvard University Press.

 1974: *The Coming of Postindustrial Society*. London: Heinemann.

Ben-David, J. 1971: *The Scientist's Role in Society*. Englewood Cliffs: Prentice-Hall.

Berg, M. 1980: *The Machinery Question and the Making of Political Economy*. Cambridge: Cambridge University Press.

Berger, P. and Luckmann, T. 1967: *The Social Construction of Reality: A Treatise in the Sociology of Knowledge*. New York: Doubleday.

Bijker, W., Hughes, T. and Pinch, T. (eds) 1987: *The Social Construction of Technological Systems*. Cambridge, Ma.: MIT Press.

Blumer, H. 1951: Social movements. In A. M. Lee (ed.). *New Outline of the Principles of Sociology*, New York: Barnes and Noble.

Boggs, C. 1985: *Social Movements and Political Power*. Philadelphia: Temple University Press.

Bookchin, M. 1971: *Post-Scarcity Anarchism*. San Francisco: Ramparts.

Bourdieu, P. 1984: *Distinction*. Cambridge, Ma.: Harvard University Press.

1988: *Homo Academicus*. Cambridge: Polity.

Boyle, G. and Harper, P. (eds) 1976: *Radical Technology*. London: Wildwood House

Branch, T. 1988: *Parting the Waters: America in the King years 1954–63*. New York: Simon and Schuster.

Byrne, P. 1988: *The Campaign for Nuclear Disarmament*. London: Croom Helm.

Carson, C. 1981: *In Struggle: SNCC and the Black Awakening of the 1960s*. Cambridge, Ma.: Harvard University Press.

Carson, R. 1962: *Silent Spring*. Boston: Houghton Mifflin.

Castles, F. 1978: *The Social Democratic Image of Society*. London: Routledge and Kegan Paul.

Chu, E. and Chubin, D. (eds) 1989: *Science off the Pedestal: Social Perspectives on Science and Technology*. Belmont, Ca.: Wadsworth.

Cohen, J. 1985: "Strategy or identity: new theoretical paradigms and contemporary social movements." *Social Research*, 52.

Commoner, B. 1966: *Science and Survival*. New York: Viking.

1972: *The Closing Circle*. New York: Bantam.

Cotgrove, S. 1982: *Catastrophe or Cornucopia: The Environment, Politics and the Future*. Chichester: John Wiley.

Cramer, J., Eyerman, R. and Jamison, A. 1987: "The knowledge interests of the environmental movement and its potential for influencing the development of science." In S. Blume et al. (eds), *The Social Direction of the Public Sciences*, Dordrecht: Reidel.

Dickson, D. 1974: *Alternative Technology and the Politics of Technical Change*. Glasgow: Fontana.

Djilas, M. 1957: *The New Class: An Analysis of the Communist System*. New York: Praeger.

Dosi, G. et al. (eds) 1988: *Technical Change and Economic Theory*. London: Frances Pinter.

Eisenstadt, S. 1966: *Modernization: Protest and Change*. Englewood Cliffs, NJ: Prentice-Hall.

Ettinger, E. 1987: *Rosa Luxemburg: A Life*. London: Harrap.

Evans, R. (ed.) 1969: *Readings in Collective Behavior*. Chicago: Rand McNally.

Evans, S. 1980: *Personal Politics*. New York: Vintage.

Eyerman, R. 1981: *False Consciousness and Ideology in Marxist Theory*. Stockholm: Almqvist and Wiksell.

1983: "Intellectuals and popular movements." *Praxis International*, 2 (3).

1984: "Social movements and social theory." *Sociology*, 18 (2).

1990: "Social movements and modernity." In N. Smelser (ed.), *Social Change and Modernity*, Berkeley: University of California Press.

Eyerman, R. and Jamison, A. 1989: "Environmental knowledge as an organizational weapon: the case of Greenpeace." *Social Science Information*, 2.

Fairclough, A. 1987: *To Redeem the Soul of America: The Southern Leadership Conference and Martin Luther King, Jr.* Athens, Ga.: University of Geovqia Press.

Feuer, L. 1969: *The Conflict of Generations*. London: Heinemann.

Feyerabend, P. 1975: *Against Method*. London: New Left Books.

Flacks, R. 1971: *Youth and Social Change*. Chicago: Markham.

Frank, A. and Fuentes, M. 1988: "World economy and social movements." Paper presented at second international Karl Polanyi Conference, Montreal.

Frankel, B. 1987: *The Post-Industrial Utopians*. Cambridge: Polity.

Freud, S. 1945: *Group Psychology and the Analysis of the Ego*. London; Hogarth. First Published 1921.

Friberg, M. and Galtung, J. (eds) 1984: *Rörelserna*. Stockholm: Akademilitteratur.

Fuller, S. 1988: *Social Epistemology*. Bloomington: Indiana University Press.

Gamson, W. 1975: *The Strategy of Social Protest*. Homewood, Ill.: Dorsey.

Garner, R. and Zald, M. 1985: "The political economy of social movement sectors." In G. Suttles and M. Zald (eds), *The Challenge of Social Control*, Norwood, N.J.: Ablex.

Garrow, D. 1987: *Bearing the Cross: Martin Luther King, Jr, and the Southern Leadership Conference*. New York: Morrow.

Gerth, H. H. and Mills, C. (eds) 1946: *From Max Weber: Essays in Sociology*. New York: Oxford University Press.

Giddens, A. 1985: *The Constitution of Society*. London: Macmillan.

Gitlin, T. 1980: *The Whole World is Watching: Mass Media in the Making and Unmaking of the New Left*. Berkeley: University of California Press.

1987: *The Sixties: Years of Hope, Days of Rage*. New York: Bantam.

Goldsmith, E. 1972: *A Blueprint for Survival*. Harmondsworth: Penguin.

Gorz, A. 1967: *Strategy for Labor*. Boston: Beacon.

1982: *Farewell to the Working Class*. London: Pluto.

Gouldner, A. 1970: *The Coming Crisis of Western Sociology*. New York: Basic Books.

1976: *The Dialectic of Ideology and Technology*. New York: Seabury.

1979: *The Future of Intellectuals and the Rise of the New Class*. New York: Macmillan.

1985: *Against Fragmentation*. New York: Oxford.

Gramsci, A. 1971: *Selections from the Prison Notebooks*. New York: International Publishers.
Habermas, J. 1972: *Knowledge and Human Interests*. London: Heinemann.
1987a: *The Philosophical Discourse of Modernity*. Cambridge: Polity.
1987b: *The Theory of Communicative Action*, vol. 2. Cambridge: Polity.
1989: *The structural transformation of the Public Sphere* (1962). Cambridge: Polity.
Hays, S. 1987: *Beauty, Health and Permanence: Environmental Politics in the United States, 1955–1985*. Cambridge: Cambridge University Press.
Heberle, R. 1951: *Social Movements: An Introduction to Political Sociology*. New York: Appleton-Crofts.
Hobsbawm, E. 1979: *The Age of Capital 1848–1875*. New York: Scirbner's.
Horkeimer, M. 1974: *Eclipse of Reason*. New York: Seabury.
Illich, I. 1973: *Tools for Conviviality*. London: Calder and Boyars.
Jacoby, R. 1987: *The Last Intellectuals*. New York: Basic Books.
Jamison, A. 1978: Democratizing technology. *Environment*, January–February.
1982: *National Components of Scientific Knowledge: A Contribution to the Social Theory of Science*. Lund: Research Policy Institute.
1987: *The Making of the New Environmental Movement in Sweden*. Lund: Research Reports, Department of Sociology.
1988: Social movements and the politicization of science. In J. Annerstedt and A. Jamison (eds), *From Research Policy to Social Intelligence*. London: Macmillan.
Jamison, A., Eyerman, R., and Cramer, J. (with Laessoe, J.) 1990: *The Making of the New Environmental Consciousness. A Comparative Study of the Environmental Movements in Sweden, Denmark and the Netherlands*. Edinburgh: Edinburgh University Press.
Jay, M. 1973: *The Dialectical Imagination*. London: Heinemann.
Jenkins, J. 1981: Sociopolitical movements. *Handbook of Political Behavior*, 4.
1989: States and social movements: recent theory and research. *Social Science Research Council Newsletter*.
Katsiaficas, G. 1987: *The Imagination of the New Left: A Global Analysis of 1968*. Boston: South End Press.
Katzenstein, M. and Mueller, C. (eds) 1987: *The Women's Movements of the US and Western Europe*. Philadelphia: Temple University Press.
Keniston, K. 1965: *The Uncommitted: Alienated Youth in American Society*. New York: Harcourt, Brace and World.
1968: *Young Radicals*. New York: Harcourt, Brace and World.
Kerr, C. 1966: *The Uses of the University*. New York: Harper and Row.

King, M. 1987: *Freedom Song*. New York: Quill.

Kingston, J. 1976: It's been said before and where did that get us? In Boyle and Harper (eds).

Kitschelt, H. 1986: Political opportunity structures and political protest. *British Journal of Political Science*, 16.

Klandermans, B., Kriesi, H. and Tarrow, S. (eds) 1988: *International Social Movement Research*. Vol. 1: *From structure to Action*. Greenwich, Conn.: JAI Press.

Knorr-Cetina, K. and Mulkay, M. (eds) 1983: *Science Observed: Perspectives on the Social Study of Science*. London: Sage.

Kołakowski, L. 1978: *Main Currents of Marxism*. Vol. 2: *The Golden Age*. Oxford: Oxford University Press.

Konrad, G. and Szelenyi, I. 1979: *The Intellectuals on the Road to Class Power*. Brighton: Harvester.

Kosik, K. 1976: *Dialectics of the Concrete*. Dordrecht: Reidel.

Kriesi, H. 1989: New social movements and the new class in the Netherlands. *American Journal of Sociology* 94 (5).

Kuhn, T. 1962: *The Structure of Scientific Revolutions* (International Encyclopedia of United Science). Chicago: University of Chicago Press.

Latour, B. 1987: *Science in Action*. Milton Keynes: Open University Press.

Latour, B. and Woolgar, S. 1979: *Laboratory Life*. London: Sage.

Law, J. (ed.) 1986: *Power, Action and Belief: A New Sociology of Knowledge?* London: Routledge and Kegan Paul.

LeBon, G. 1960: *The Crowd*. New York: Viking – First published 1985.

Lenin, N. 1977: *What Is to be Done?* In *Selected Works*, vol. 1, Moscow: Progress Publishers. First published 1902.

Lepenies, W. 1988: *Between Literature and Science: The Rise of Sociology*. Cambridge: Cambridge University Press.

Lipset, S. (ed.) 1967: *Student Politics*. New York: Basic Books.

Lipset, S. and Dobson, R. 1972: The intellectual as critic and rebel: with special reference to the United States and the Soviet Union. *Daedalus*, 101, summer.

Lowe, P. and Goyter, J. 1983: *Environmental Groups in Politics*. London: Allen and Unwin.

Lukács, G. 1972: *Tactics and Ethics*. London: New Left Books. First published 1918.

McAdam, D. 1982: *Political Process and the Development of Black Insurgency, 1930–1970*. Chicago: University of Chicago Press.

 1988: *Freedom Summer*. New York: Oxford.

McCarthy, J. and Zald, M. 1973: *The Trend of Social Movements in America*. Morristown, NJ: General Learning Press.

Malcolm X 1966: *Autobiography*. London: Hutchinson.

Mallet, S. 1976: *Essays on the New Working Class*. St Louis: Telos Press.

Mannheim, K. 1948: *Ideology and Utopia*. London: Routledge and Kegan Paul.

Marcuse, H. 1964: *One-Dimensional Man*. Boston: Beacon.
  1969: *An Essay on Liberation*. Boston: Beacon.
Martin, B. and Szelenyi, I. 1987: Beyond cultural capital: toward a theory of symbolic domination. In R. Eyerman et al. (eds), *Intellectuals, Universities, and the State in Western Modern Societies*, Berkeley: University of California Press.
Maslow, A. 1962: *Toward a Psychology of Being*. New York: Van Nostrand.
  1964: *Religions, Values and Peak-Experiences*. Columbus: Ohio State University Press.
Melucci, A. 1985: The symbolic challenge of contemporary movements. *Social Research*, 52.
  1988: Social movements and the democratization of everyday life. In J. Keane (ed.), *Civil Society and the State*, London: Verso.
  1989: *Nomads of the Present*. Philadelphia: Temple University Press.
Merton, R. 1957: *Social Theory and Social Structure*. New York Free Press.
Merz, J. 1965: *A History of European Thought in the Nineteenth Century*, vol. 1. New York: Dover. First published 1896.
Michels, R. 1959: *Political Parties*. New York: Dover.
Miller, J. 1987: *Democracy is in the Streets*. New York: Simon and Schuster.
Mills, C. Wright 1959: *The Sociological Imagination*. New York: Oxford University Press.
  1963: *Power, Politics and People*. New York: Ballantine Books.
Mitchell, R. 1979: Since *Silent Spring*: science, technology and the environmental movement in the United States. In H. Skoie (ed.), *Scientific Expertise and the Public*, Oslo: Norwegian Research Council for Science and the Humanities.
Mommsen, W. and Osterhammel, J. (eds) 1987: *Max Weber and his Contemporaries*. London: Allen and Unwin.
Morris, A. 1984: *The Origins of the Civil Rights Movement*. New York: Free Press.
Nelkin, D. 1977: Scientists and professional responsibility: the experience of American ecologists. *Social Studies of Science*, 7 (1).
Noble, D. 1983: Present tense technology. *Democracy*, 1.
O'Brien, J. 1983: Environmentalism and a mass movement: historical notes. *Radical America*, 17 (2–3).
Offe, C. 1985: New social movements: challenging the boundaries of institutional politics. *Social Research*, 52, winter.
Olofsson, G. 1987: After the working class movement? An essay in what's 'new' and what's 'social' in the new social movements. *Acta Sociologica*, 31 (1).
Olson, M. 1965: *The Logic of Collective Action*. Cambridge, Ma.: Harvard University Press.

Paehlke, R. 1989: *Environmentalism and the Future of Progressive Politics*. New Haven: Yale University Press.

Parkin, F. 1968: *Middle Class Radicalism*. Manchester: Manchester University Press.

Parsons, T. 1969: *Politics and Social Structure*. New York: Free Press.

Pepper, D. 1984: *The Roots of Modern Environmentalism*. London: Croom Helm.

Piven, F. and Cloward, R. 1977: *Poor People's Movements*. New York: Pantheon.

Reich, W. 1972: *Sex-Pol*. New York: Vintage.

Ridgeway, J. 1970: *The Politics of Ecology*. New York: E. P. Dutton.

Rootes, C. 1978: The rationality of student radicalism. *Australian and New Zealand Journal of Sociology*, 14 (3).

  1980: Student radicalism: politics of moral protest and legitimation problems of the modern capitalist state. *Theory and Society*, 9 (3).

  1982: Student radicalism in France: 1968 and after. In P. Cerny (ed.), *Social Movements and Protest in France*, London: Frances Pinter.

Rose, H. and Rose, S. (eds) 1975: *The Radicalisation of Science*. London: Macmillan.

Ross, A. 1989: *No Respect: Intellectuals and Popular Culture*. London: Routledge.

Rucht, D. 1988: Themes, logics and arenas of social movements: structural approach. In Klandermans et al. (eds).

Rudig, W. 1988: Peace and ecology movements in Western Europe. *West European Politics*, 11, January.

Ryle, M. 1988: *Ecology and Socialism*. London: Century Hutchinson.

Sale, K. 1974: *SDS*. New York: Vintage.

Scheler, M. 1980: *Problems of a Sociology of Knowledge*. London: Routledge and Kegan Paul. First published 1924.

Schumacher, E. 1973: *Small is Beautiful: Economics as if People Mattered*. London: Blond and Briggs.

Shorter, E. and Tilly, C. 1974: *Strikes in France, 1830–1960*. New York: Cambridge.

Smelser, N. 1962: *Theory of Collective Behavior*. New York: Free Press.

Taylor, R. and Young, N. (eds) 1987: *Campaigns for Peace*. Manchester: Manchester University Press.

Therborn, G. 1976: *Science, Class and Society*. London: New Left Books.

Thompson, E. 1966; *The Making of the English Working Class*. New York: Vintage.

Tilly, C. 1978: *From Mobilization to Revolution*. Reading, Ma.: Addison-Wesley.

  1985: Models and realities of popular collective action. *Social Research*, 52, winter.

Tilly, C., Tilly, L. and Tilly, R. 1975: *The Rebellious Century*. Cambridge, Ma.: Harvard.

Toulmin, S. 1982: *The Return to Cosmology: Postmodern Science and the Theology of Nature*. Berkeley: University of California Press.

Touraine, A. 1977: *The Self-Production of Society*. Chicago: University of Chicago Press.

1981: *The Voice and the Eye: An Analysis of Social Movements*. Cambridge: Cambridge University Press.

1983: *Anti-Nuclear Protest*. Cambridge: Cambridge University Press.

1988: *The Return of the Actor*. Minneapolis: University of Minnesota Press.

Turner, R. and Killian, L. 1957: *Collective Behavior*. Englewood Cliffs: Prentice-Hall.

Weart, S. 1988: *Nuclear Fear*. Cambridge, Ma.: Harvard University Press.

Weber, M. 1958: *The Protestant Ethic and the Spirit of Capitalism*. New York: Scribners.

1978: *Economy and Society*. 2 vols, Berkeley: University of California Press.

Webster, C. 1975: *The Great Instauration: Science, Medicine and Reform 1626–1660*. London: Duckworth.

Zald, M. and McCarthy, J. 1987: *Social Movements in an Organizational Society: Collected Essays*. New Brunswick: Transaction.

# Index